The Church

The Church

Glorious Body, Radiant Bride

Banner Mini-Guides
Key Truths

Mark G. Johnston

THE BANNER OF TRUTH TRUST

THE BANNER OF TRUTH TRUST

Head Office
3 Murrayfield Road
Edinburgh, EH12 6EL
UK

North America Office
PO Box 621
Carlisle, PA 17013
USA

banneroftruth.org

© The Banner of Truth Trust, 2018
First published 2018
Reprinted 2020

ISBN
Print: 978 1 84871 809 8
EPUB: 978 1 84871 810 4
Kindle: 978 1 84871 811 1

*

Typeset in 10/14 pt Minion Pro
at the Banner of Truth Trust, Edinburgh

Printed in the USA by
Versa Press, Inc.,
East Peoria, IL

Contents

To

John and Deborah Woolley

Introduction

Despite the many sources of information that exist about 'church', there is only one that can genuinely claim to define what the church is and how it ought to function. And, even though it leaves room for different interpretations as to what this may look like in practice, it alone provides all that we need to know about this subject. That source is, of course, the Bible.

Were it not for this 'revelation' from God—in the Old Testament as much as in the New—one person's view of church would be of no more value than another's. But when we begin to explore what God has to say on this theme, we ought to be thrilled, intrigued, challenged and ultimately transformed by what we see.

The very first book I read on this subject was *Cinderella with Amnesia* by Michael Griffiths.[1] I was a teenager at the time and the title immediately grabbed my attention. It conjured up the image of a princess who had forgotten who she was and what rightfully belonged to her. It well portrayed the sad reality of the church—the 'princess bride' of Christ—and what she so often forgets. Only when the people of God rouse themselves from the ashes of their own

[1] Leicester: IVP, 1975.

misconceptions will they truly discover what the church is and is meant to be. Above all, they will see it as the 'glorious body' and 'radiant bride' of the Lord Jesus Christ. As that happens, they will begin to experience what John Newton referred to as the 'solid joys and lasting treasure' which 'none but Zion's children know'.[1]

A book of this size cannot possibly treat this great subject in much detail. The doctrine of the church has filled the pages of many large volumes. This is a 'mini-guide', one of a series that will introduce the reader to some of the major themes and issues related to the Christian faith. Each one will provide an outline of the Bible's teaching on a particular subject. They will open up a key verse or portion of Scripture for study, while not neglecting other passages related to the theme under consideration. The goal is to whet your appetite and to encourage you to explore the subject in more detail: hence the suggestions for further reading which appear after the final chapter. However, the mini-guide will provide enough information to enlarge your understanding of the theme.

All the mini-guides have been arranged in a thirteen-chapter format so that they will seamlessly fit into the teaching quarters of the church year and be useful for Sunday School lessons or Bible class studies.

One of the things Christians soon discover about the church is the extent to which it shapes our lives as we are touched and blessed by the fellowship of brothers and

[1] From the hymn 'Glorious Things of Thee Are Spoken' by John Newton (1725–1807).

sisters in Christ. Two people whose lives have made a deep impression on me and my family over the years are John and Deborah Woolley. They were our close friends and neighbours in London for much of the time we spent there, and latterly they have been very much part of our life in Cardiff. We have also had the pleasure of their company as members of our church, in which John has served with me as a dear brother and colleague in ministry. It is my pleasure to dedicate this book to them.

MARK G. JOHNSTON
Cardiff
January, 2018

1

The Church and Why It Matters

1 Peter 2:4-12

The church of Jesus Christ is making her presence felt in a remarkable way in many parts of the world. In the Far East, India, Africa, and South America it is growing so rapidly that it is difficult to train sufficient numbers of pastors and teachers to instruct the new converts and care for their spiritual needs. In many countries the ruling authorities are taking notice of the church's increasing strength and influence and in too many places repressive measures have been introduced in an attempt to discourage the church's growth. In other parts of the world, however—most notably in the West where once it was strong—the church appears to be a great irrelevance. Regardless of whether the church is expanding or shrinking, the great question we cannot ignore is: *What is the church and why does it matters?*

It may be tempting to approach the question from a sociologist's or perhaps from some other specialist's perspective; but such approaches have inbuilt limitations, not least a prior denial of the supernatural. How can one even begin to understand the church without at least a recognition that there is a God, and that he not only exists, but is also at work in the world he has made? We need to go back to the 'charter document' of the church, for in it we will discover an altogether different insight into this subject.

A quick survey of the Bible will show us just how dominant a theme the church is within its pages. Indeed, it is impossible to read the Bible without coming to the conclusion that the church occupies a central place in God's great plan of salvation for the world.

We can see this very clearly in the first letter of Peter. Peter was an apostle of the Lord Jesus Christ, and he wrote this letter to Christians who were 'dispersed' throughout the regions of Asia Minor. He speaks of them as 'exiles' (1 Pet. 1:1). This is a most interesting word for it has more than one meaning. By using it Peter may simply be reminding his readers of the spiritual truth that they, as Christians, are 'resident aliens', people who live in one country (in this case, Asia Minor) but who really belong to another (in the Christian's case, heaven, cf. Phil. 3:20). But Peter's use of the term may point to another important fact. Many Christians at that time were displaced persons or refugees who had fled their homelands in order to find safety elsewhere. This sad circumstance may have been uppermost in Peter's mind for only a few verses later he writes about the 'various trials' his readers had endured (1 Pet. 1:6). It is fair to say that Peter wrote his letter at a time when the church and its members were experiencing serious opposition and even persecution from the Roman authorities.

It is not hard to imagine the doubts and fears that must have troubled and unsettled these 'exiles' who, in the eyes of the world, were a despised and marginalized people. Peter's letter was written to encourage and strengthen their faith. His message to them is: 'Remember your true identity. You are the people of God.' In carefully chosen words the apostle turns their attention away from their low standing in the eyes of the world to their high standing in the sight of God. 'You matter to God!' is the truth he wants them to realize. Notice how Peter sets it before them in such a way as to highlight the great importance of church.

Chosen and precious

First of all he reminds them of their true identity *in Christ*. 'As you come to him, a living stone rejected by men but in the sight of God chosen and precious, you yourselves like living stones are being built up as a spiritual house, to be a holy priesthood' (1 Pet. 2:4, 5).

The '*him*' referred to here is the 'Lord' (2:3), that is, 'our Lord Jesus Christ' (1:3). It is in union with him that they have 'tasted' or experienced God's goodness in salvation (cf. Psa. 34:8).

The truth of the Christian's union with Christ has several important implications. Every Christian, and especially suffering Christians, ought to be aware of them. One is this: we are united to a person who was 'rejected by men'. It should not surprise us, therefore, if we experience the same rejection Jesus suffered at the hands of the world. But the other side of this truth is also applicable to us: we are united to one who is 'in the sight of God chosen and precious'. That which is true of Christ is also true of all those who are united to him by faith. We may be despised and rejected by men on account of our allegiance to Jesus, but in him we are 'in the sight of God chosen and precious'!

An important point Peter is making in this chapter is this: Jesus is the foundation stone on which the church is built, and since he is supremely special to God, the same must be true for all the 'living stones' that are being built on him.

This chapter is a good place to begin our exploration of the Bible's teaching on the church. It is also a most relevant passage for us because we too live in a world that is just as hostile to the church of Jesus Christ.

It is vitally important, then, that we see the church, not as the world sees it, from a merely human point of view; but as God sees it, in the pure light of his word.

What image springs to mind when you hear the word 'church'? Do you think of the bricks and mortar of ecclesiastical buildings, whether medieval cathedrals or small whitewashed meeting houses? That is not how God sees the church. The Scriptures teach that the church is the people whom God has called into a special relationship to himself through his Son. Or to put it in a slightly more theological form: the church is the people whom God has brought into a covenant relationship with himself.

The word 'covenant' is not commonly used today, but it was well understood in Bible times and was used in all kinds of ways. For example, when nations related to each other under the 'international law' of that period, or when deals were sealed in commercial transactions, the term 'covenant' was often employed. The word also expressed the special relationship between a man and a woman in marriage. The concept of *covenant marriage* is one that often appears in the Bible to portray the way in which God relates to his people.[1] *Covenant* conveys the idea of a spiritual marriage between God and his people—a living, loving, and legally binding relationship.

At the heart of this covenant bond is the truth revealed in words spoken by God through his Old Testament prophet Jeremiah: '*I will be their God, and they shall be my people*' (Jer. 31:33). Notice that God is the one who will do the binding! '*I will be their God*': he will bind himself to his people, not the other way round. In the gospel we see the unimaginable lengths to which God went in order to bring this covenant relationship into being: the covenant was sealed and secured by the blood of Jesus Christ, his one and only Son (cf. Luke 22:20; 1 Cor. 11:25).

---

[1] See, for example, the message of the Song of Solomon which, at one level, is a poetic celebration of the love between a man and a woman, but at another, celebrates the bond between Christ and his people. We see it too in the prophecy of Hosea which laments the breakdown of this special relationship—at a human level in the prophet's own marriage, but more tragically in the way God's people were guilty of spiritual adultery. But the passage that most clearly spells out this relationship is Ephesians 5:21-33, where Paul speaks about marriage and the profound mystery of the bond between Christ and the church.

God's new humanity

In the next few verses of his letter Peter uses extraordinary language to describe the 'exiles' to whom he was writing. His terms are all the more staggering when we remember that his original readers felt themselves to be a small, persecuted, and despised minority. Yet he says of them:

> But you are a chosen race, a royal priesthood, a holy nation, a people for his own possession, that you may proclaim the excellencies of him who called you out of darkness into his marvellous light. Once you were not a people, but now you are God's people; once you had not received mercy, but now you have received mercy.
>
> (1 Pet. 2:9, 10)

Almost every syllable of these two verses is drawn directly from the Old Testament and was originally used to describe God's old covenant people Israel—the church of that epoch in God's plan of redemption.[1] Israel was more than a mere earthly nation; the people of Israel were a tangible expression of God's new humanity in a fallen world.

In one sense Old Testament Israel was the focus of these references. But here they are used to describe the church of the New Testament era, which had as many if not more Gentile than Jewish members. God's 'chosen race' and 'holy nation' is now made up of people from every ethnicity who have been called 'out of darkness and into his marvellous

---

[1] In the *Septuagint* (or LXX—the ancient Greek translation of the Hebrew Bible), the word *ecclesia* (church) is used to translate *qahal*, the Hebrew word for 'sacred assembly' which was used of Israel when gathered in worship (see, e.g., Deut. 9:10; 10:4; 18:16).

light'. This fact is a fulfilment of the promise made to Abraham, the father of the nation of Israel, when God entered into a covenant with him. God said to him:

> I will make of you a great nation,
>> and I will bless you and make your name great,
>> so that you will be a blessing.
> I will bless those who bless you,
>> and him who dishonours you I will curse,
> and *in you all the families of the earth shall be blessed.*
>> (Gen. 12:2-3)

In order to grasp the implications of this more fully, we need to take a step even further back in time. Long before Abraham was born God had a people on earth: we can trace them all the way back to the Garden of Eden. They are those who placed their trust in God and who 'called upon the name of the Lord' (cf. Gen. 4:26).

It was in Eden that some of the most significant words in the entire history of the human race were spoken. Immediately after the fall of Adam into sin, when God pronounced judgment on our first parents because of their rebellion against him, God made a wonderful promise. It was spoken within the context of God's judgment upon the serpent (Satan) who had tempted Eve to take of the forbidden fruit. God said: 'I will put enmity between you and the woman, and between your offspring and her offspring; he shall bruise your head, and you shall bruise his heel' (Gen. 3:15). The 'offspring' or 'seed' (the word in the original Hebrew is singular) of the woman pointed forward to a man who would come and do all that was necessary to 'undo' all the disastrous consequences of Adam's sin. That 'seed' of the woman was Jesus of Nazareth who was also the eternal Son of God.

This is the truth that the apostle Paul taught to the Galatian Christians: 'But when the fullness of time had come, God sent forth his Son, born of woman … to redeem …' (Gal. 4:4-5). The Son of God took to himself our humanity in order to bring deliverance to the world. Later, writing to Titus, a colleague in the work of the Christian ministry, Paul sums up the whole purpose of Jesus' saving mission by saying that he 'gave himself for us to redeem us from all lawlessness and *to purify for himself a people for his own possession* who are zealous for good works' (Titus 2:14). In other words, God sent his Son into the world so that through his life, death, resurrection, and exaltation he might bring forth a new humanity out of the wreckage of the old humanity that had been ruined by Adam's fall into sin.

Peter wanted his readers to realize that they were part of God's new, redeemed humanity—the church of Jesus Christ. Even though far from perfect, they belonged to a whole new order of being through their union with Christ. And the same is true of us if we are believers too!

Belonging to a different world

Peter concludes this section of his letter with a word of exhortation for his fellow Christians:

> Beloved, I urge you as sojourners and exiles to abstain
> from the passions of the flesh, which wage war against
> your soul. Keep your conduct among the Gentiles hon-
> ourable, so that when they speak against you as evildoers,
> they may see your good deeds and glorify God on the
> day of visitation (1 Pet. 2:11, 12).

Peter's readers must grasp the fact that they belong to a different world, to God's redeemed world, on account of their union with Christ. It is precisely because they are 'sojourners and exiles'—that is, citizens of heaven who are temporarily resident in this world—that they must live in a way that is morally and spiritually counter-cultural to the world around them. Though they are *in* the world, they are not *of* it. They belong to a different world altogether! The citizens of heaven follow the customs and laws of the heavenly country to which they belong.

This helps us to understand why the world despises the church and dismisses it as of no consequence. But when Christians see the church as God sees it, as we view it through the lens of Scripture, we discover that, far from being of no consequence, the church is as precious to God as his own Son. Since the church matters so much to God, it should matter a great deal to us as well.

2

The Church and God's Wisdom

Ephesians 3:10, 11

Critics have sometimes parodied the church as 'a ship of fools',[1] in order to dismiss those who belong to it and who uphold its beliefs as beneath the dignity of reason.

The Bible takes a very different view. It rises above the realm of human wisdom to that of God himself, and shows how the church fits into his wise dealings with the world he has made. Paul refers to this in his letter to the church in Ephesus.

But before we look at what the apostle says directly about the church and the wisdom of God, we should note a few preliminary things about his letter to the Ephesians.

Although all New Testament letters expound the same message—the gospel of the Lord Jesus Christ—each does so in response to a particular situation facing the church. In the case of the Christians in Ephesus, it was their pressing need to grasp the very idea of 'church' itself. Paul wrote

---

[1] An expression borrowed from Plato, the Greek philosopher (*c.* 424–328 B.C.).

his letter to explain what the church really is and how it ought to function.

As the number of Gentile converts increased in Ephesus, some of the old tensions between Jews and Gentiles began to appear within the church, creating all kinds of problems. Rather than deal with each problem individually, Paul went straight to the root cause of the division to provide a full and comprehensive solution. In our next chapter we will look at the issue more closely, but in this chapter we shall focus on how the church is spoken of here as the object through which God displays his perfect wisdom.

Paul refers to God's wisdom directly when he tells his readers 'that through the church the manifold wisdom of God might now be made known to the rulers and authorities in the heavenly places. This was according to the eternal purpose that he has realized in Christ Jesus our Lord' (Eph. 3:10, 11). This brief statement says a lot more than we might at first realize. Let us break it down into its component parts and take a closer look at its teaching.

Planned from eternity

Paul has been speaking about 'the mystery' that 'was made known to [him] by revelation' (Eph. 3:3). The word 'mystery' is an important technical term in the New Testament. It does not refer to something that is mysterious or mystical; rather it is used of something that is beyond the reach of human investigation but which has been made known by God through special revelation.

Jesus Christ and the apostles he had chosen (including Paul) were God's agents or instruments in the final phase of his self-revelation to the world (Eph. 3:4, 5; cf. John 17:6-8; Heb. 1:1-3).

In this passage, as Paul addresses the situation that had arisen in Ephesus, he focuses on one aspect of the divine mystery: 'that the Gentiles are fellow heirs, members of the same body, and partakers of the promise in Christ Jesus through the gospel' (Eph. 3:6). In other words, God's great salvation was never intended to be restricted to the nation of Israel but was for all the nations of the world.

This may not sound like a major issue to us, but for Christians living in New Testament times, who had come to faith in Christ from either a Jewish or Gentile background, the idea of being brought into a close relationship with people from other religious and ethnic groups was almost unthinkable. Indeed, for the Ephesians, it was *the* issue that was threatening to tear their church apart.

God's answer to this division between human beings is the gospel of his Son, the Lord Jesus Christ. Christ's death on the cross is the means by which God makes 'peace' for both Jew and Gentile: through the death of Jesus, God 'has made … both one' and 'has broken down … the dividing wall of hostility' that had kept them apart from time immemorial (Eph. 2:14). Now Paul wants his readers to see how God's saving work in Christ displays the divine wisdom in a way that eclipses even God's wisdom in his works of creation and providence. Hence the breathtaking claim in this third chapter of Ephesians.

What especially deserves our attention here is the adjective 'manifold' which is used to describe God's wisdom (3:10). Paul uses a word in the original Greek that could be translated 'multifaceted' or 'multicoloured'. It carries the idea of a kaleidoscope of complex beauty. God's 'manifold wisdom' will never cease to amaze those who seriously consider it. It is displayed most strikingly in the church, in the collective life of those who are drawn together from otherwise divided, and even hostile, communities. By God's grace real peace and harmony is experienced in his new community.

All of this was central to God's plan from eternity. It was, says Paul, 'according to the eternal purpose' of God (Eph. 3:11). Far from being an afterthought on God's part, the uniting of Jew and Gentile in Christ was something he had planned from before the beginning of time. Through the cross, God would reconcile sinful people not only to himself, but also to one another. If Christ's death was the means by which the ultimate divide between the holy God and sinful people was healed, then how much more will it be the remedy for the much smaller-scale divisions which mar the human race!

Secured in history

It should go without saying that everything God purposed in eternity will be fulfilled in time. This is true not just in relation to the myriad details of human history, from the little things of personal life to epoch-making world events, but supremely true in the one event that changed everything. That was, of course, the coming into the world of the Son of God, including all that he accomplished as Saviour of the world. What God had planned in his kaleidoscopically detailed wisdom 'he has realized in Christ Jesus our Lord' (Eph. 3:11).

When we read this statement against the backdrop of what Paul has already said, it becomes clear that Christ's death is key to the success of his saving mission on earth. That is why the cross is central to all that Paul has said in the previous chapter. The cross was that critical moment in history which sealed destinies—for good or ill—for all eternity. When Jesus cried out on the cross 'It is finished' (John 19:30), a glimpse was given into his decisive achievement at Calvary. This was no cry of defeat, but a shout of victory. An alternative translation makes this even clearer: 'It is accomplished!' Jesus had perfectly completed all the work that the Father had given him to do. Salvation was secured for all his people.

Displayed universally

Arguably the most astonishing thing in Paul's letter to the Ephesians is his portrayal of the church as the object in which God's wisdom is most gloriously seen. It is through the church primarily that God displays his wisdom to 'the rulers and authorities in the heavenly places' (Eph. 3:10).

Who are these 'rulers and authorities'? Later in his letter they are referred to again when Paul warns the Ephesians of the evil and dark powers which the devil marshals in his warfare against the church—'the rulers … the authorities

… the cosmic powers over this present darkness … the spiritual forces of evil in the heavenly places' (Eph. 6:12). But in chapter 3 the apostle is surely also including the good angels and heavenly beings as well as the evil ones. The good 'angels', Peter tells us, long to 'look into' the outworking of God's saving plan (1 Pet. 1:12). Paul tells us that a day is coming when 'at the name of Jesus every knee should bow, *in heaven* and *on earth* and *under the earth*, and every tongue confess that Jesus Christ is Lord, to the glory of God the Father' (Phil. 2:10, 11). It will not just be the good angels and all of the redeemed who will glorify him in this way; even those who rejected Christ will pay him homage, as will the devil and his angels. The former will acknowledge Christ as Lord willingly with joy, but the latter will do so under duress with grief. But the point is clear: that day will surely come, and the church will be centre-stage in the drama.

There is, then, a sad irony that the world has chosen Plato's moniker 'ship of fools' to mock the church. It is a sarcastic echo of the church's claim to be the 'ark of salvation'. But just as Noah's neighbours lampooned him as a fool for building the ark that would save him from the coming flood, only for them to perish in their own folly, so will it be for those who despise the church. They will discover, but only too late, that 'the foolishness of God is wiser than men' (1 Cor. 1:25).

3

The Church as God's New Community

Ephesians 1:1-14

The destruction of community is one of the devastating effects of sin. In the beginning, when the human race was just a community of two (Adam and Eve), division entered the world hot on the heels of sin. When God questioned Adam with respect to his eating the forbidden fruit, the man laid the blame for his actions on his wife: 'The woman … gave me … and I ate' (Gen. 3:12). Later, following their expulsion from the Garden and the birth of their children, this little family was torn apart by envy, anger, and murder.[1] It is a sad fact that from its earliest days on earth the human race has been all too familiar with social fragmentation.

The Bible draws attention to this very deliberately. In Genesis 6 it shows us a race destroying itself by rampant, unrestrained wickedness. So extreme had the situation become that God brought an apocalyptic judgment upon the world by means of a great flood, which was also a

---

[1] See the story of Cain and Abel in Gen. 4:1-8.

sobering display of divine wrath and an indication of the final judgement that awaits all evil. But against this dark backdrop of judgment we also see the light of God's mercy: 'But Noah found favour in the eyes of the LORD' (Gen. 6:8).

The story is well known. God saves Noah and his family from the waters in the ark and gives them a new start when the flood waters have receded from the face of the earth. But as the story continues, we see once again the strong grip of sin on the human heart. Sin brings division into Noah's family and judgment on one of his three sons, and just two chapters later we read the account of the Tower of Babel and the scattering of the nations (Gen. 11:1-9). The race that was meant to be one glorious, harmonious community is now divided and dispersed over the face of the whole earth as a result of sin. And the rest, as the saying goes, is history.

Day after day, at every level of society, we see broken relationships. Nation rises against nation; nations divide along social, ethnic, and political lines. The divisions even reach down to the most basic expression of community life in the family. Families are torn apart by marital breakdown, separation, and divorce. Division has become so pervasive that we may be tempted to say: 'That's the way it has always been, and thus it will ever be!' But is that so?

One of the glorious features of the Christian gospel is that it offers an alternative to this depressing fact of life. It tells us that God has gone to extraordinary lengths to save his people from their sins, and to ensure that their new life in this world will be very different. God's purpose is to restore what sin has ruined. Nowhere is that more true than in the shared life of the only creatures that were made in his image and likeness—men and women.

Paul's letter to the Ephesians speaks with particular relevance to this issue. The church in that city was itself suffering from deep and bitter divisions. As we noticed in the previous chapter, the church's members came from both Jewish and Gentile backgrounds. Despite their new life in Christ, some had brought the baggage of their pre-Christian past into the church. As a result all the prejudice and bigotry that had bred centuries of hostility between Jews and Gentiles was threatening the health and peace of this Christian church.

Paul wrote to address this issue—not merely to treat the symptoms, but to tackle the underlying cause. He wants to apply the gospel in such a way to show that Christ's saving work really does heal division.

It is fascinating to see how Paul approaches the problem. He does not start with their present condition. Instead he turns their attention to a much greater reality—to God's plan which he devised before the beginning of time. In his breathtaking introduction to the letter Paul reveals God's eternal purpose for his people and how it relates to God's new community in Ephesus.

For the praise of his glory

The opening section of chapter 1 is noteworthy for several reasons. For a start, verses 3 to 14 are remarkable in terms of their literary composition. Although they are neatly arranged into separate sentences in our English versions, they constitute one long single sentence in Paul's original Greek! But at a deeper level (which may explain the phenomenal nature of this 'breathtaking' sentence), Paul takes us into the sheer wonder of God's plan of salvation and its fulfilment in Christ. With a striking turn of phrase he reveals the purpose for which God has redeemed his people and formed them into a new community—all has been done '*to the praise of his glory*' (1:12).

The apostle uses the same language, with slightly different nuances, at other points in the passage. The 'adoption' that brings us into God's family is '*to the praise of his glorious grace*' (1:6).[1] Then, at the end of the section, where he speaks of believers being 'sealed with the promised Holy Spirit', all of this saving work, he says, is '*to the praise of his glory*' (1:14).

This refrain plays a significant role in Paul's opening statement. Was not the problem at Ephesus closely bound up with certain factions within the church seeking glory for themselves? Indeed it was! In particular, those of Jewish extraction tended to regard their Gentile fellow church members as second-class citizens of God's kingdom and not worthy of its full benefits. Perhaps these Jewish

[1] The fact Paul uses the Greek word *huiothesia* 'adoption as sons' here should not make us think that God is biased towards males. Rather, Paul, under the inspiration of the Holy Spirit, chose this word deliberately to address a mixed audience of men and women in order to show that the privileges of sonship, which were denied to daughters in Roman families, were freely given to women as well as men in God's family.

Christians would not let the Gentile believers forget that under the old order of things Gentiles were 'alienated from the commonwealth of Israel' and were 'strangers to the covenants of promise' (Eph. 2:12). But Paul makes it crystal clear that things are very different now. He tells the Gentile believers in this church: 'But now in Christ Jesus you who once were far off have been brought near by the blood of Christ' (Eph. 2:13).

The blood of Christ that reconciled God to alienated human beings also reconciles sinful people who are alienated from one another. The cross tears down the old barriers of culture, prejudice, and outright hostility. In Christ they are no longer divided but at one with each other as equal members of God's new community. 'There is neither Jew nor Greek, there is neither slave nor free, there is neither male nor female, for you are all one in Christ Jesus' (Gal. 3:28).

Could there be a more visible display of the gospel's power to change lives? The bringing together of believing Jews and Gentiles into the one fellowship of the church was an eloquent testimony to God's saving purpose and redounded 'to the praise of his glorious grace'.

Through the word of truth

It is one thing to see God's declared purpose for the church in what he has decreed from eternity; it is another thing to see how it is achieved. But Paul proceeds to explain that as well.

His explanation focuses on the words 'in Christ'. This little phrase is Paul's favourite way of speaking about a Christian and he uses it extensively throughout his letters. It conveys the truth of the believer's 'union with Christ'—the new relationship that transforms absolutely everything.

To help us grasp its significance let us think about what happens at that moment in a marriage ceremony when the happy couple say 'I do'. As they join their lives together, all the assets and liabilities of one become the other's. The same is true in our relationship to Christ, the exception being that he only gets our liabilities while we receive his assets! This is the wonderful new reality into which we enter when we receive God's salvation as a free gift.

There is, however, another aspect to this. How do we become aware of all that Christ is and has done for us? How are we brought into a personal experience of his salvation? Paul answers those questions by telling his readers: 'In him you also, when you heard the word of truth, the gospel of your salvation, and believed in him, were sealed with the promised Holy Spirit' (Eph. 1:13). God's revealed word and the good news it contains are the means by which we are brought to know Christ and to receive by faith the salvation which he alone provides.

Paul puts an even finer and more astonishing point on this when he says a little further on in his letter: 'he came and preached peace to you who were far off and peace to those who were near' (Eph. 2:17). The astonishing thing about that statement is the fact that he (that is, Jesus) never physically visited Ephesus. How, then, can Paul say that Jesus came and preached to them? The staggering answer is that through the preaching of the word by Paul, Christ spoke to the Ephesians (cf. Eph. 6:20; 2 Cor. 5:20).

It is also striking that Paul speaks of this within the context of the church being built up as God's new community. The gospel not only brings people to new life in Christ, it also builds them up together as the church grows and matures. Paul picks up this theme in his letter to the Romans. He tells the Christians in that great city not to be shaped any longer by the pattern of this world, but instead to be continually transformed *by the renewing of their minds* (Rom. 12:2). This transforming renewal only comes as the mind is exposed to the sanctifying truth of God's word (cf. John 17:17). Christians do not grow in a 'mystical' way without any thought or effort on their part. No, they grow only as they receive the word of God and respond to it with 'the obedience of faith' (cf. Rom. 1:5; 16:26).

Sealed by the Holy Spirit

The best of communities are fragile. Families fracture, nations decline, institutions collapse. Sadly the same may be true of churches. A cursory reading of the New Testament will show that none of the churches in those days were perfect and none of them were spared the experience of broken relationships within the fellowship. How, then, can Christians be sure that what they have in Christ is going to survive?

Building on what he has just said about the role that God's word plays in bringing people to faith and building them up as his new community, Paul goes on to speak of the role of the Holy Spirit: 'you also … were sealed with the promised Holy Spirit, who is the guarantee of our inheritance until we acquire possession of it, to the praise of his glory' (Eph. 1:13, 14). God seals with the Holy Spirit those whom he has called to himself and united to his Son.

A 'seal' was a common feature of commercial and legal transactions in the ancient world. When something needed to be certified and guaranteed a seal was applied. It was a mark of its authenticity and a guarantee of quality. The Holy Spirit is God's seal on the believer. He who indwells all believers is the divine guarantee that Christ has given them eternal life and that they shall never perish (John 10:28).

Paul expresses a similar idea in his letter to the church in Philippi. He declares his total confidence that the God who began a good work in them 'will bring it to completion at the day of Jesus Christ' (Phil. 1:6).

Two thousand years of church history are testimony to the way God has honoured this Holy Spirit guarantee. The new community he is building in his Son has been preserved and will continue to grow until the end of time.

4

The Church as the Body of Christ

1 Corinthians 12:12-31

The Bible uses a number of different images to portray the church of God. In the Old Testament, for example, the covenant nation of Israel is described as God's 'vine' (Psa. 80:8-16; Isa. 5:1-7; Jer. 2:21; Ezek. 15:1-8; 17:5-10; 19:10-14; Hos. 10:1). Jesus takes that image and uses it to illustrate his relationship to the church. He is 'the true vine' and only by remaining in him will the church produce the fruit that God desires to see (John 15:1-17). Paul borrows another Old Testament picture of Israel's relationship to God when he speaks of the church as the 'bride' of Christ (Eph. 5:22, 33). This beautiful image of the church is later used by John in the book of Revelation (Rev. 19:6-9; 21:2, 9). Elsewhere the church is said to be Christ's 'flock', God's 'family' and 'household', and even God's 'field' (John 10:16, 26; Acts 20:28; 1 Pet. 5:2; 1 Tim. 3:15; Heb. 3:6; 1 Pet. 4:17; 1 Cor. 3:9). All of these images show us that the church is a living thing, animated by the spiritual life that comes from God himself.

The Bible also uses other word-pictures to describe the church and how it functions. Since these have more to do with organization and structure, they may seem at first to be of a different order. Peter, for example, speaks about the church as God's 'temple', composed of 'living stones' (1 Pet. 2:4-5); John portrays it as a 'city' (Rev. 21:2, 10-27), and as 'seven golden lampstands' (Rev. 1:20); while Paul speaks of it as a 'pillar and buttress of truth' (1 Tim. 3:15).

Though different, these two perspectives of the church are not contradictory. Rather, they complement each other and help us understand a reality which no single image can adequately set forth. Some of the images used, however, such as Peter's reference to the church as a temple built with living stones, indulge a delicious mixing of metaphors.

There is another passage which does this ever so well. It is found in Paul's first letter to the church in Corinth—another church that was deeply troubled. Its organic life had come under enormous strain as a result of internal divisions (1 Cor. 1:10-12), and its order, especially in its public worship, had become somewhat chaotic (1 Cor. 14:26-33, 40). It is both interesting and illuminating to notice that when Paul provides specific teaching on what the church is and how it ought to function, he uses imagery that brings together the two perspectives mentioned above. He wants the Corinthians to realize that the church is both *a living organism* and *a structured organization*.

If we see the church in this light and appreciate the link between these two perspectives we will be able to counter some of the extremes that have frequently injured the church and its reputation. It will also prevent us from viewing the church as a mere institution on the one hand, and as a body with an undisciplined life of its own on the other.

The apostle teases out these thoughts in some detail. With real pastoral insight he explains the nature of the church as 'the body of Christ'.

A living organism

In 1 Corinthians 12 Paul speaks of the church as *a body* (1 Cor. 12:12, 27). He has already used this metaphor earlier with reference to the Lord's Supper and the Corinthians' abuse of that sacrament. He points to the close connection between the actual body of Christ represented by the bread in the Supper and the gathering of Christians into one 'body' in either a local congregation or in the wider church (1 Cor. 10:17). Such is the union between Christ and his people collectively that the apostle speaks of them interchangeably.

This understanding of the connection between Christ and his church was clearly stamped on Paul's consciousness the day when the risen Christ took hold of him. He was on his way to Damascus to persecute the church when, just outside the city, Jesus stopped him in his tracks with these words: 'Saul, Saul, why are you persecuting *me*?' (Acts 9:4, 5). Paul may have been tempted to retort: 'Jesus, I'm not persecuting you, but the church!' But he knew only too well that the charge was true.

The connection between Christ and his church is reflected in the instructions Paul gives the Corinthians regarding the

Lord's Supper (1 Cor. 11). In a deliberately nuanced statement he first tells them: 'Whoever, therefore, eats the bread or drinks the cup of the Lord in an unworthy manner will be guilty of profaning the body and blood of the Lord' (1 Cor. 11:27). The Corinthians must see their abuse of the Supper as an offence against the Christ who is offered in it.

But he also goes on to say: 'For anyone who eats and drinks without discerning the body eats and drinks judgment on himself' (1 Cor. 11:29). Here Paul picks up on the metaphor used in the previous chapter about the church as the body of Christ. The disrespect some members of the Corinthian church were showing to their fellow church members (1 Cor. 11:17-22) they must now see for what it really was: it was disrespect for Christ their Lord.

This background helps us appreciate why Paul reaches for the same metaphor a third time in chapter 12 and develops it further. For although the issue under consideration has now moved from the abuse of the Lord's Supper to the misuse of the gifts of the Holy Spirit, the context is exactly the same—the Corinthians' utter failure to grasp the true nature and glory of the church *as the body of Christ*. All division in the church, and all of the trouble and pain that flow from it, stem from this great underlying failure.

In the first part of chapter 12 Paul reminds the believers in Corinth that though there are different kinds of spiritual gifts, there is just one body and one Holy Spirit. He develops this thought by employing the analogy of a body with many parts which is animated by one spirit (1 Cor. 12:12-13). The analogy helps us to see not only the diversity that exists within the church (the many parts), but also the unity of the church (one body, animated by one spirit). The church is alive. It is animated by the shared life of the Holy Spirit.

Each part of the body is important. No matter how insignificant or even embarrassing a particular body part may seem, it is nevertheless integral to the body, and is part of it for a reason (1 Cor. 12:14-20). Each part is so intimately connected to all the others that one part's pain or pleasure will be felt by all the others (1 Cor. 12:21-26).

So, then, the church is a living body. Its members are brought together, not merely because of a shared interest or a common cause, but because of the spiritual life they share in the Lord Jesus.

A structured organization

As Paul rounds off this section of his letter, he takes his teaching a step further. He reaffirms what the members of the church are together and how each one makes a vital contribution to the well-being of the whole: 'Now you are the body of Christ and individually members of it' (1 Cor. 12:27). Then he goes on to speak about the various spiritual gifts and graces that shape their shared life and enable them to function effectively as one.

He mentions a range of gifts given by the Holy Spirit for the church at that time (1 Cor. 12:28). Some were special gifts just for that period when the church was being established in the world, such as the working of miracles and speaking in other tongues (or languages). Such gifts were given to attest the arrival of the final phase of God's plan of redemption. Salvation had been secured and was now to be proclaimed to the ends of the earth. There were also foundational gifts in the church at that time, such as apostles and prophets, who were used by God to complete his written word, what we now call 'the New Testament'. They also had a unique role in establishing the template the church was to follow until the return of Christ.

Two other gifts mentioned in this passage—of teaching and administration—were permanent features of the church. Both were vitally important for leadership.

The life of the church was not left to 'grow wild'. The Spirit who gives life to the people of God is not a Spirit of unpredictable spontaneity. He leads and directs the church by the word of God and in keeping with what God has revealed about his character. That is why 'order' and 'peace' should be characteristic marks of the church, 'for God is not a God of confusion but of peace' (1 Cor. 14:33). Hence Paul's maxim: 'all things should be done decently and in order' (1 Cor. 14:40).

A people living in harmony

There is one other important detail to notice in Paul's teaching about the church. It is an easy one to miss because of the unfortunate division between chapters 12 and 13 of 1 Corinthians. It is this: *love must be ever-present in the life of the church*. Love is the 'more excellent way' referred to at the end of chapter 12.

Only by love will the diverse community of the Corinthian church (or any other church for that matter!) be able to live harmoniously and function properly. Sound structures and efficient administration are good but not sufficient of themselves; they can never be a substitute for this essential ingredient for church life. This love is disciplined and intentional in expression. It is self-sacrificing and persevering, just like the love of God displayed in Christ (1 Cor. 13:4-7). It is governed not by mere feelings but by a tender-hearted, conscious commitment to others. Love is the badge of the true Christian, for as Jesus told his disciples in the Upper Room: 'By this all people will know that you are my disciples, if you have love for one another' (John 13:35).

5

The Church and the Sacraments

Romans 4:11

Baptism and the Lord's Supper have been key features of the church's life from New Testament times.

The Lord's Supper, as its name suggests, is not a human invention, but the Lord's gift to his people. On the night Jesus was betrayed he shared one last Passover meal with his disciples. During the meal he gave the familiar Old Testament rite a whole new significance (Matt. 26:17-30). What is sometimes referred to as the 'Last Supper' became the first Communion service of the church. It was to be the first of many for this sacramental meal which the Lord instituted on that memorable night is to be observed again and again 'until he comes' (1 Cor. 11:26).

The sacrament of baptism is also the Lord's gift to the church. Although there were various 'baptisms' or ritual washings in Old Testament times, and although John baptized in the early days of the New Testament period, it was the Lord Jesus who ordained *Christian* baptism. This, uniquely, is to be administered 'in the name of the Father and of the Son and of the Holy Spirit' (Matt. 28:19).

It is a sad fact that throughout church history the meaning and significance of these precious gifts have been a matter of argument and bitter strife between Christians. The Lord's Supper was the focus of major conflict around the time of the Protestant Reformation. Baptism has long been a matter of dispute among Protestants who have not been able to reach a consensus on the mode[1] and subjects[2] of this sacrament. It is both tragic and ironic that the very things which Christ gave his church as tangible expressions of unity have become occasions of division.

Though it is tempting to shy away from this subject, the issues at stake are too important to neglect. The Bible portrays the church as a sacramental community and it is vital that we see the significance of this.

Seeing the sacraments in context

Baptism and the Lord's Supper are special, not only because they were given to the church by the Lord Jesus Christ, but because they were given within the context of God's covenant with his people. The living, loving, and legally-binding covenant bond is God's unbreakable commitment to his people in a spiritual marriage.[3]

In the past God attached certain signs to the covenants he established with his ancient people. In the covenant with Noah the sign was the rainbow (Gen. 9:12-17); in the

---

[1] That is, immersion in water only; or immersion, pouring, or sprinkling.

[2] That is, believers only; or believers and their children.

[3] Cf. my remarks in chapter 1.

covenant made with Abraham, the sign was circumcision (Gen. 17:1-14); and in the covenant made with the nation of Israel at Sinai, the sign was the Sabbath (Exod. 31:13). As in the Old so in the New, God has provided something tangible for believers in Jesus to hold on to as signs and seals of his new covenant.

We can see a hint of this in Paul's letter to the Romans where, in connection with the covenant made with Abraham, he speaks of a 'sign' and a 'seal' being given to the patriarch:

> He received the *sign* of circumcision as a *seal* of the righteousness that he had by faith while he was still uncircumcised. The purpose was to make him the father of all who believe without being circumcised, so that righteousness would be counted to them as well (Rom. 4:11).

Circumcision was the sign of God's covenant with Abraham. The sign pointed to the God who had made the promise; it was God's pledge that he would keep his word.

The Westminster divines of the seventeenth century borrowed these scriptural terms when they drew up their chapter on the sacraments in the *Confession of Faith*. They spoke of baptism and the Lord's Supper as 'signs and seals of the covenant of grace'.[1] Baptism and the Lord's Supper signify certain key aspects of gospel salvation. Cleansing from sin, union with Christ, the new birth, and the new life in Christ are all signified or portrayed in the sacrament of baptism. The Lord's Supper sets forth the death of Christ

---

[1] *Westminster Confession of Faith*, XXVII.1.

as the ground of our salvation, 'the Bread of Life' by whom we are spiritually nourished, and to the shared life believers experience in union with him.

However, baptism and the Lord's Supper are more than signs; they are also 'seals of the covenant of grace', and they serve to assure us that God will keep his word and do what he has promised. They are designed to make us certain of his covenant faithfulness.

Baptism

There is a natural order to the sacraments: baptism first, then the Lord's Supper. Baptism is the sacrament that is linked to our entry into the church. The Lord's Supper is the communal meal of those who are members of the church.

Baptism was ordained by the risen Lord Jesus Christ who commanded his church to practise it to the end of the age (Matt. 28:18-20). It has been a feature of the church's life and witness since the Day of Pentecost (Acts 2:38, 39). Baptism features prominently in the teaching of the New Testament, which is a clear indication of the important place it ought to occupy in our understanding of salvation.

Baptism has its roots in the Old Testament. Circumcision was the rite of initiation administered to the sons of Abraham, marking them out as members of the people of God. It is clear from what Jesus said (Matt. 28:19) and from what Peter preached (Acts 2:38) that baptism is the new rite of initiation that replaces circumcision. This can also be seen in Paul's letter to the Colossians in which he links the symbolism of both circumcision and baptism to the great reality of what it means to be savingly united to Christ (Col. 2:11, 12).

Since baptism has replaced circumcision as the rite of initiation into the church, both the uncircumcised (Gentiles) and the circumcised (Jews) were brought into the new community of God's people through this sacrament. This 'missionary baptism', administered to those who publicly profess their faith in Christ (but who have not been baptized before), continues to be practised wherever the gospel is preached to 'unchurched' people.

Many churches teach that this is the only form of baptism. They say that there is no command given to baptize infants and there are no examples of infants being baptized in the New Testament.

Other churches, however, hold to a different position. They see continuity between the Old and the New Testaments with respect to the core beliefs and practices of the church. The Old Testament passages that speak of God's covenant include references to the children of believers having a place in God's covenant dealings with his people. For that reason the children of believers are to receive the sign of the covenant. When Peter preaches his sermon on the Day of Pentecost his words of application contain loud echoes of the covenant promises of the Old Testament and, it is argued, a repetition of the place of children within the community of God's new covenant people.

All the leaders of the mainstream Protestant Reformation and the majority of their successors in the Puritan movement of the following century believed the children of believers should be baptized. But whatever position one adopts on this subject, all recognize that baptism is an important part of church life because it is a sacrament which the Lord Jesus Christ ordained. He gave it to his church as a solemn pledge that the good work he began, he will complete on his return (Phil. 1:6).

The Lord's Supper

The special meal which Jesus instituted on the eve of his crucifixion is described in various ways in the pages of the New Testament, each of which has helped to shape the church's understanding of it.

In the early chapters of Acts it is referred to as 'the breaking of bread' (Acts 2:42). Luke, the author of Acts, used this expression to identify the special meal that, along with the apostolic teaching, fellowship, and prayer, constituted the core components of the Jerusalem church's life. Very likely, during this early phase of the New Testament church, the Lord's Supper was an extension of the fellowship meals or love feasts of that period (Acts 2:46). However, as the church grew in its appreciation of Christ's teaching, so its understanding of the significance of the Supper deepened.

It is also referred to as the Lord's Supper (1 Cor. 11:20); the Lord's Table (1 Cor. 10:21); Communion (from the term 'participation', 1 Cor. 10:14-22; and Jesus' graphic description of how we commune with him in John 6:53-58); the Eucharist (from the Greek verb *eucharisteo* which means to give thanks; Jesus gave thanks before administering the first Supper, 1 Cor. 11:24). Each term helpfully conveys a different dimension of this sacrament.

The Lord's Supper has been the occasion of controversy in the long history of the church. Four distinct views have been put forward which seek to explain the nature of the Supper and how it benefits those who receive it. Here is a very brief summary of the four views:

The Roman Catholic Church teaches the doctrine of 'transubstantiation'. It believes that the body and blood of Christ are physically present in the bread and wine. When the priest consecrates the elements in the Supper, it is claimed that the so-called '*substance*' of the bread and wine is changed into the 'body, blood, soul, and divinity' of Jesus Christ. The medieval Catholic Church formally approved the doctrine of transubstantiation in 1215. It promotes the belief that Jesus Christ is offered up as an 'unbloody' sacrifice each time the Mass is celebrated. This doctrine became one of the key theological battlegrounds of the sixteenth-century Reformation. The Protestant Reformers were right to vigorously condemn the Mass as a degrading denial of the finished work of Christ, and as promoting the idolatrous worship and adoration of the bread and wine.

Three other views of the Lord's Supper emerged within Protestantism.

First, the Lutheran Church, seeking to distance itself from Rome's view of the Supper, embraced the doctrine of 'consubstantiation' in relation to the way Christ is related to the elements. Instead of their *becoming* his actual body and blood, Christ was believed to be present 'in, with and under' the elements. This was an attempt to do justice to the words of Jesus: 'This *is* my body' (Matt. 26:26). But its great weakness is its failure to safeguard the Bible's teaching on the nature of Christ's humanity. In order to maintain the link between Christ's physical body and the elements of bread and wine, Lutherans spoke of the 'ubiquity' of Christ's body—that it is everywhere present. But the inescapable implication of such teaching was that the human nature of Jesus Christ was somehow constitutionally different from the rest of the human race. If Jesus was not 'made like his brothers in every respect' (sin excepted), then how could he could be our representative and Saviour (cf. Heb. 2:17)?

Second, Ulrich Zwingli, the Swiss Reformer of Zurich, explained the Lord's Supper in a way that distanced himself from the Lutheran view. While affirming that Christ is indeed present in the sacrament, he tended to understand that as an extension of Christ's promise to be present wherever two or three were gathered together in his name (Matt. 18:20). He thought of the Supper as a present testimony to the past accomplishment of Christ's death. He believed that its benefit came through the power of the word preached as part of its celebration. Other Reformers, not least John Calvin, disagreed with this view, arguing that it fails to capture the full weight of the language used of the Supper both in the Gospels and in Paul's letters.

Third, the dominant view to emerge from the Reformation, and the one reflected in the confessions of many Protestant churches, is that Christ is really present and at work in the Supper by his Holy Spirit and through his word. In this covenantal meal Christ is pleased to impart himself to his people. At the Supper believers 'feed upon him in their hearts by faith with thanksgiving'.[1] Such a view also helps to make sense of the stark warnings linked to the Lord's Supper (1 Cor. 11:29).

Much more could be said on all the points covered in this chapter. But suffice to say we cannot properly appreciate the church without appreciating just how much baptism and the Lord's Supper matter in its life, worship, and witness.

[1] *The Book of Common Prayer.*

6

The Church and Its Worship

Hebrews 12:22-24

Worship has always been characteristic of the people of God. When God created man he made him in his own 'image' and 'likeness' (Gen. 1:26, 27). The chief end of God's image-bearers was 'to glorify God and to enjoy him forever.'[1] Human nature was programmed to worship God. But when sin entered the world at the fall, the programme became corrupted. Human beings are still worshippers; but since the fall they 'worship and serve the creature rather than the Creator' (Rom. 1:25).

The word 'godly', which occurs frequently in the Bible, means to be 'godlike'. It is the will of God that all his children are godly (1 Thess. 4:3): this is good and pleases God (1 Tim. 2:3); to 'live … godly lives in the present age' is also one of the reasons why the saving grace of God appeared (Titus 2:11, 12). God wants to reproduce his holy character in his people.

For this reason Paul appeals to the Roman Christians to 'present [their] bodies as a living sacrifice, holy and

[1] *Westminster Shorter Catechism*, Question 1

acceptable to God, which is [their] spiritual worship' (Rom. 12:1). He also teaches the Ephesians that the great purpose of God's saving work in Christ was that 'we who were the first to hope in Christ might be to the praise of his glory' (Eph. 1:12).[1] Simply being what we are called to be in Christ is the foundation of all true worship. This is an important consideration, for it will guard our worship from being mechanical and outward. True worship is the overflow of a renewed heart.[2]

A time and place

When God created the world he set apart the Garden of Eden as a specially designated area in his perfect world. Here he would meet with his people. A pattern was established in the Garden that was continued through the progressive stages of Old Testament history: it is seen in the lives of the patriarchs who built altars 'to the LORD' and who 'called upon the name of the LORD'. It is also seen after the nation's exodus from Egypt when Israel built the tabernacle in the wilderness under Moses' leadership; and then again, long after Israel's settlement in Canaan, they built the temple in Jerusalem under Solomon's supervision. So although God's image-bearers were to honour their Creator at all times, there were also special times and ways in which God was to be worshipped. This can be seen in the account of creation given in Genesis. Though every day of the week

---

[1] This theme has been treated more fully in chapter 3.
[2] See, for example, Isa. 29:13.

was a God-given day, nevertheless one day in seven was set apart as 'holy' and 'blessed' by God. The Sabbath is his special day. This one-day-in-seven pattern of worship has been part of the DNA of God's people from the beginning of time. God calls his people to worship him on the day he has given and set apart for that purpose.

This is the backdrop to the verses we shall consider in Hebrews 12. The author of this letter was writing to Jews who had come to faith in Jesus. They had suffered much because of their faith. In fact, things had become so difficult for them that they were being tempted to go back to the old religion they had once shared with their Jewish relatives, friends, and neighbours. In this climactic section of the letter, the author opens up to their view the sheer wonder of new covenant worship in the Lord Jesus Christ. His teaching will help us understand what it means to belong to God's worshipping community.

The context of worship

He begins by reminding his readers of what it was like to worship the God who entered into covenant with Israel at Mount Sinai (Exod. 19:1-25). Their experience of God at Sinai was wonderful but also terrifying (Heb. 12:18-21). Then he contrasts that with the way worship has been transformed and brought into a whole new dimension by the coming of Christ.

Notice how the writer draws the contrast between *then* and *now*. He says: 'For you have not come to what may be touched, a blazing fire and darkness and gloom and a tempest … *But* you have come to Mount Zion and to the city of the living God, the heavenly Jerusalem' (Heb. 12:18, 22).

There is a *heavenly* and there is an *earthly* Jerusalem. The temple in Jerusalem must be seen for what it truly was: a 'man-made sanctuary', a mere earthly 'copy and shadow of the heavenly things' (Heb. 8:5; cf. Exod. 25:8, 9, 40). The *real* sanctuary is in heaven.

It was this real sanctuary that Jesus entered and where he continues to minister. How different is this to the ministry of all the priests of the old covenant who served in either tabernacle or temple! 'Christ,' we are told, 'has entered, *not into holy places made with hands*, which are copies of the true things, *but into heaven itself*, now to appear in the presence of God on our behalf' (Heb. 9:24).

The implications of this statement are far-reaching and open up to us wonderful new horizons of worship. Jesus Christ takes his believing people far beyond the mere symbols, types, and shadows of the temporary arrangements of the old covenant and into the great permanent reality of new covenant worship.

Such an insight was a much-needed corrective for the first readers of this letter. Given the circumstances in which they found themselves, it was easy for them to become discouraged, especially when their humble places of worship were compared with the grandeur of the Jerusalem temple. But, as the writer has already reminded them, they are to 'live by faith' (Heb. 10:38); and faith is 'the conviction of *things not seen*' (Heb. 11:1). So whether they meet for worship in an upper room, or in a private house, or 'in deserts and mountains, and in dens and caves of the earth' (Heb. 11:38), the author wants them to know that at the same time they come 'to Mount Zion and to the city of the living God, the heavenly Jerusalem'. What a thought!

Moreover, the Hebrew Christians were not merely gathering with a few despised fellow worshippers on earth; he tells them that 'innumerable angels in festal gathering' were also part of their congregation, as was the entire 'assembly of the firstborn who are enrolled in heaven', and 'the spirits of the righteous made perfect' (Heb. 12:22, 23). Above all, God was present, for they had 'come … to God'. Though he is 'the judge of all', yet he accepted them because they had come to 'Jesus, the mediator of a new covenant, and to the sprinkled blood'. Jesus the mediator ushered them into the Father's presence (Heb. 12:23, 24).

This 'faith-perspective' is something every Christian needs. It will transform everything, not least the place of the church's weekly gatherings: whether that be a temple (Acts 3:1), a riverside (Acts 16:13), a rented lecture hall (Acts 19:9), or an upper room (Acts 20:8), the earthly meeting place is entirely incidental and ultimately insignificant.

It was this same truth that Jesus taught to the Samaritan woman by the well at Sychar (John 4), although he applied it in a different way. She had raised an issue which had long been a source of strife between Samaritans and Jews: where was the true and proper place to worship God? She had said to Jesus: 'Our fathers [the Samaritans] worshipped on this mountain [Mount Gerizim], but you [Jews] say that in Jerusalem is the place where people ought to worship.' But Jesus said: 'Woman, believe me, the hour is coming when neither on this mountain nor in Jerusalem will you worship the Father. ... God is spirit, and those who worship him must worship in spirit and truth' (John 4:20, 21, 24). Worship is not a matter of geography but theology! Reflecting on this truth the hymn-writer penned these beautiful words:

> Jesus, where'er Thy people meet,
>   There they behold Thy mercy-seat;
> Where'er they seek Thee Thou art found,
>   And every place is hallowed ground.
>
> For Thou, within no walls confined,
>   Inhabitest the humble mind;
> Such ever bring Thee when they come,
>   And, going, take Thee to their home.[1]

The key to worship

As we think through this passage in Hebrews it will become clear to us that the person and work of the Lord Jesus Christ is the key to authentic worship. He is 'the mediator' (Heb. 12:24). A mediator bridges the great divide between estranged parties. Jesus brings together, or reconciles, God and those who have rebelled against him. This work cost him his own precious blood.

The author here speaks of this 'blood' in Old Testament terms: it has been 'sprinkled' and 'speaks a better word than

[1] William Cowper (1731–1800).

the blood of Abel'. The blood of murdered Abel cried out for vengeance on the one who slew him; the blood of Jesus calls out for mercy. Did he not pray 'Father, forgive them, for they know not what they do' for those who nailed him to the cross?[1] The 'blood of Christ' is that which has the power to 'purify our conscience from dead works' so that we can 'serve the living God' (Heb. 9:14).

Worship is supremely Christ-conscious. Although God-centred, it is saturated with an awareness that the only way we can come to God, be accepted by him, and enjoy fellowship with him is through the one and only mediator, the Lord Jesus Christ (cf. 1 Tim. 2:5).

That is a truth not everyone is happy to accept. Perhaps that is the reason behind the author's blunt warning: 'See that you do not refuse him who is speaking' (Heb. 12:25). God has spoken (Heb. 1:1, 2), but through his written word he still speaks.

This reminds us of how serious a thing it is to hear the word of God. When we hear it we must respond immediately. But implicit in these words is the truth that all we need to know about God, including how we are to approach him in worship, is contained in Holy Scripture.

The pattern for worship adopted by the early Christians was widely known throughout the churches of the New Testament period. The first converts 'devoted themselves to the apostles' teaching and fellowship, to the breaking of bread and the prayers' (Acts 2:42). These four things are

[1] Luke 23:34.

sometimes referred to as 'the means of grace', that is, the ways in which God graciously engages with his people. They are the core elements of worship that please God: the reading and preaching of the word of God, the fellowship of believers, the sacraments of baptism and the Lord's Supper, and prayer in its various forms. The Holy Spirit uses each in our communion and fellowship with Christ, and through him with God the Father.

The ethos of worship

The author of Hebrews adds one other comment at the end of this section that is both salutary and thought-provoking. He says that we are to 'offer to God acceptable worship, with reverence and awe, for our God is a consuming fire' (Heb. 12:28, 29). The adjective *acceptable* implies that there are expressions of worship that God will not accept. The description of God as 'a consuming fire' should make it abundantly clear that we should never approach him carelessly, thoughtlessly, or lightly. If the sinless angels in heaven bow their heads before God's majestic holiness, and cry, 'Holy, holy, holy is the Lord of hosts', then how much more should we, who are but dust and ashes, worship him 'with reverence and awe'!

7

The Church and Its Mission

Matthew 28:19-20

M ission has always been integral to God's purpose for his people. In the first formal statement of his intent, God made clear his purpose to bless 'all the families of the earth' through Abraham (Gen. 12:3).

Although Abraham would be the father of the nation of Israel, he would also be the father of many nations, as people from all ethnic backgrounds put their faith in Abraham's God (Rom. 4:12, 16, 17). Israel should have been a 'missionary' nation—'a light to the nations' (Isa. 60:1-5)— had it understood the terms of God's covenant promise. The author of Psalm 67 was perhaps one of the few Israelites who realized this when he wrote: 'May God be gracious to us and bless us and make his face to shine upon us, *that your way may be known on earth, your saving power among all nations*'. His heart's desire was: 'Let the peoples praise you, O God; let *all the peoples* praise you!' (Psa. 67:1-3). Mission did not begin with the Great Commission.

Though Israel was not the model of missionary outreach she ought to have been, it is nevertheless marvellous to see the Gentiles who did find refuge under the wings of the God of Israel. They included among others Rahab[1] and Ruth,[2] both of whom became part of Jesus' family tree (see Matt. 1:5). It is also wonderful to see how the reputation of the God of Israel was enhanced on the international stage through the godly influence of outstanding Hebrews such as Joseph (who became the prime minister of Egypt), Daniel (the prime minister of Babylon), and Esther (the Queen of Persia).

The church in the New Testament era experienced extraordinary missionary success. An indicator of that success can be seen in an incident that took place shortly after Paul and Silas arrived in the northern Greek city of Thessalonica. The two 'missionaries' were dragged before the authorities by an angry crowd who accused them of having 'turned the world upside down' by their preaching of the gospel (Acts 17:6). In just one generation the gospel went from the extremities of the Empire to the very heart of Rome. There were even those in Caesar's household who had become disciples of Jesus (Phil. 4:22).

However, the story of missionary expansion of the church is not one that we can be totally proud of. The church's mission has sometimes been politicized, even militarized, and all too often marginalized. But one thing is clear: mission has always been part of God's purpose for

---

[1] Rahab was a prostitute in Jericho who was kind to the Israelite spies. See Josh. 2.

[2] Ruth was from the land of Moab. She had married an Israelite. When her husband died, she took care of her widowed Jewish mother-in-law Naomi in the land of Israel. See Ruth 1-4.

his covenant people. Nowhere is that more clearly affirmed than in the last words Jesus spoke to his disciples before his ascension into heaven (Matt. 28:19, 20; Luke 24:46-48; Acts 1:8). They have been called 'the marching orders of the church'.

The right to bear witness

Notice the precise wording of the Great Commission. Jesus says, 'Go therefore and make disciples of all nations' (Matt. 28:19). The word 'therefore' demands our attention. It points to the astonishing statement Jesus made in the previous verse: 'All authority in heaven and on earth has been given to me.' Here is the reason the disciples are to make disciples of all the nations.

Imagine if Jesus had never made that statement. What if the disciples just heard him say: 'Go and make disciples of all nations.' How do you think they would have reacted? Would they not have asked, 'What right have *we* to do that?' After all, who were they to undertake such a task? They were nobodies. They were not trained in the officially validated institutions of their day; they had not been ordained by the religious establishment. Had they not already discovered from the example of Jesus that their warrant to speak God's message in God's name was going to be open to challenge (cf. John 7:48)? But Jesus 'came and said to them, "All authority in heaven and on earth has been given to me. Go therefore …"' Their mandate to preach the gospel to the world and to make disciples of all nations came from the very highest authority!

This 'authority' was given to Jesus by the Father as his reward for the completion of the work he had been given to do for the salvation of his people (cf. John 17:4, 5). Because the Son 'made himself nothing' by 'taking the form of a servant' and by 'being born in the likeness of men'; because he became 'obedient to the point of death, even death on a cross', 'God has highly exalted him' (Phil. 2:5-11). It was this exaltation that Peter referred to on the Day of Pentecost when, at the conclusion of his sermon, he said to the Jews in Jerusalem: 'God has made him both Lord and Christ, this Jesus whom you crucified' (Acts 2:36).

The successful accomplishment of his mission on earth gave Jesus a new and glorious status. He is God's Saviour-King, the one who inherits the throne of universal dominion. The apostles saw in this the fulfilment of the prophetic words of Psalm 110, in which ancient Israel's King David wrote: 'The Lord says to my Lord: "Sit at my right hand until I make your enemies your footstool"' (Psa. 110:1; cf. Acts 2:34, 35).

It is this authority of the risen Christ that guarantees the success of the church's mission. 'He must reign until he has put all his enemies under his feet' (1 Cor. 15:25). The church can go into all the world with the assurance that—

> His name for ever shall endure;
> last like the sun it shall:
> Men shall be bless'd in him, and bless'd
> all nations shall him call.
>
> (Psa. 72:17, *Scottish Psalter*, 1650)

We do well to remember where the church's warrant for mission is to be found—not in its members or in the church as an institution, but in her Lord Jesus Christ.

The essence of mission

What, then, is the church's mission in the world to be? To help us answer that question we need to see beyond the way most of our English Bible versions translate these verses. For instance, the word 'go' appears to be an imperative in our English versions, giving the impression that the 'going' is the most important thing. But in the original Greek the imperative is 'make disciples'. This is the key element in the mission Jesus entrusted to his church. The church's mission, therefore, is not merely to get the gospel out to the world, nor even to win converts, important though these things are. Rather, it is to 'make disciples of all nations'. The church is always to be in 'discipling mode' if it is to fulfil its responsibility.

Mission is the responsibility and task of *the church* since the command is given to 'baptize' the newly made disciples. But individual Christians have no right to baptize new believers, neither do mission agencies. The same should be noted with respect to the 'teaching' and 'obedience' which are necessarily involved in the making of '*disciples*'. The church has been given the responsibility to ensure that the gospel is faithfully taught to and understood by its converts, who are to come under the spiritual care and supervision of the pastor-teachers Christ has given to his church.

The scope of the church's mission is to make disciples 'of all nations'. Churches should not limit the horizons of their missionary efforts. The gospel must be taken to the very ends of the earth (cf. Acts 1:8; 13:47).

The New Testament provides a challenging insight into how this great work began and provides us with a valuable paradigm for how it should continue. If we follow the story told in the Acts of the Apostles of how the gospel spread we will see clearly how Jesus' words were wonderfully fulfilled: 'You will be my witnesses *in Jerusalem* and *in all Judea and Samaria*, and *to the end of the earth*' (Acts 1:8). Here is the 'road map' of the church's mission.

Though the work of spreading the gospel was undertaken by the apostles and involved some specially-gifted evangelists as well as pastor-teachers who did the work of evangelists (cf. Eph. 4:11; 2 Tim. 4:5), we must not overlook the vital role 'ordinary' Christians played in the work. The responsibility to evangelize belonged to them as well as to church leaders. The believers who fled from Jerusalem when the first major persecution of the church took place 'went about preaching the word' (Acts 8:4). Wherever they went they evangelized, spreading the gospel message. This was not something the apostles discouraged. In fact, many years later, Peter instructed the readers of his letter—who, as we saw in an earlier chapter, were suffering because of their faith—to be always 'prepared to make a defence to anyone who asks you for a reason for the hope that is in you' (1 Pet. 3:15). Every church member is part of the church's missionary team!

The promise of his presence

Before we leave this passage we must take note of the apprehension the disciples felt as they tried to process Jesus' instructions. Matthew has already told us of the doubts of some of the disciples when they saw Jesus (Matt. 28:17). Surely they must have been anxious and fearful as they received this daunting task from their Lord. The Gospels tell us that when Jesus sent them out on previous missions, their fears were palpable. But now as then, Jesus promised to help them (cf. Luke 9:1-6; 10:1-23).

Taking the gospel to the world has always been fraught with difficulty. Jesus told his disciples that he was sending them out 'as lambs in the midst of wolves' (Luke 10:3). He warned them that 'if they persecuted me, they will also persecute you' (John 15:20). How, then, could the disciples—or those who would take up the baton of missionary service after them—overcome their fears with respect to the risks and dangers involved?

Jesus answers that question with a most encouraging promise: 'And behold, I am with you always, to the end of the age' (Matt. 28:20). The one who by his incarnation is *Immanuel*—'God with us'—will not forsake his disciples when he leaves them to ascend into heaven. He is and ever will be our Immanuel! For even though he will no longer be *physically* present on earth, he will be just as real—and even more wonderfully real!—to all his disciples *because of the ministry of the Holy Spirit* (cf. John 16:7). And the Lord says he will be with them (literally) 'all the days'—through the 'good' days and the 'bad' days too! And as they preach the gospel he will work with them to confirm his word (Mark 16:20).

Church history is full of examples of how the Lord Jesus overcame the fears and anxieties of his disciples and enabled them to bear witness to the truth of his word. The gospel has been spread across the globe by generations of faithful Christians who have taken the terms of the Great Commission seriously. Some of them, like Paul, did not count their lives precious to themselves (Acts 20:24), and gladly bore their witness by a martyr's death. Yet the Lord worked with them to confirm his word so that countless men and women, boys and girls would come to faith in Jesus Christ and become his disciples. Wherever the gospel has gone, churches have been established. Could we have any clearer proof that all authority in heaven and on earth has been given to our Lord and Saviour?

8

The Church and Its Unity

John 17:20-26

Samuel Stone's line, 'By schisms rent asunder, by heresies distressed',[1] is a sad but all-too-true summary of the church's history. From the great division of Israel into Northern and Southern Kingdoms (1 Kings 12:1-33), to the 'many' who had 'gone out' from the churches under the apostle John's care (1 John 2:19), the unity of God's people has frequently been assaulted.

Schisms never come without casualties. People are affected, friendships and even family ties are damaged, and the fellowship of God's family is disrupted. Moreover, the pain experienced in these situations is often aggravated by the knowledge that divisions may be caused by the eagerness of sincere Christians who are zealous to uphold God's truth. But, perhaps, the greatest tragedy is the damage done to God's name and the church's reputation.

The frequency and force of the Bible's teaching on this subject, coupled with the pain and embarrassment arising

---

[1] From the hymn 'The Church's One Foundation', Samuel Stone (1839–1900).

from the disruption of the church's life, has often focused the concern of God's people on unity. But ironically even this too has been a catalyst for division, especially when unity is sought at any price. Such a 'unity' has more to do with church politics and outward appearances than genuine spiritual oneness. The attempt to bring churches together on superficial grounds led one church leader to describe it as little more than 'holding hands in the dark'.[1]

Scripture speaks of a very different kind of unity. The seventeenth chapter of John's Gospel is vital for an under-standing of the kind of unity God desires for his people. The chapter records what has often been referred to as Christ's 'High Priestly prayer'. Jesus was to offer *himself* as a sacrifice for the sins of God's people the very next day, and so he prays that his sacrifice will accomplish its intended purpose.

He prays that his death on the cross would bring glory to himself and to his Father. He also prays that his death would secure the salvation of all his people (John 17:1-5).

Then he prays for his apostles, the men who had received the word of God from him and who would take the good news of salvation to the world (John 17:6-19).

However, it is the closing section of the prayer—in which Jesus prays for all those who will believe in him through the apostles' message (John 17:20-26)—that shows most clearly his concern for the church, and especially her unity.

---

[1] Alan Gibson, *Holding Hands in the Dark* (St Albans: British Evangelical Council, 1988).

What kind of oneness?

There can be no doubt about the kind of unity Jesus requests for his church: 'that they may all be one, just as you, Father, are in me, and I in you, that they also may be in us … that they may be perfectly one even as we are one, I in them and you in me, that they may become perfectly one' (John 17:21-23). Here we see the true nature of the oneness of the church. It is the same kind of oneness that exists within the Godhead, the Holy Trinity—the unity of the three persons of the Father, the Son and the Holy Spirit.

When we see the unity of the church through this lens, we realize that it belongs to an order all of its own. It transcends the unity of a common interest and a common cause. This unity is something that goes even deeper than the shared DNA that binds us together within our own human families.

The unity of the Godhead is perfect in diversity. The church is to be a reflection of that unity. God's purpose in the death of his Son Jesus was to redeem a people for himself out of every nation, tribe, people, and language (cf. Rev. 7:9). God is creating out of the vast diversity of the human race a new 'holy nation' (1 Pet. 2:9), the members of which will be united to each other because they are all united to Christ.

Such unity is not to be confused with uniformity. The Father, the Son and the Holy Spirit are three distinct persons within the Godhead; but that in no way diminishes the perfect unity and harmony in which the distinct persons exist. Therefore, as the good news of God's salvation reaches into every corner of the world and into every stratum of society, the church's members will reflect the communities from which they are drawn by the gospel. The church will never be bland or monochrome.

Unity in Christ, through his Spirit

The kind of unity for which Jesus prayed must have seemed as much the stuff of dreams to the first disciples as it does to many who read the words of John chapter 17 today. The Twelve had struggled to maintain even a semblance of unity during the three years Jesus had been with them (e.g. Mark 9:34; 10:35-41). How then could the church display this kind of oneness after his return to heaven?

The mutual indwelling of the Father and Son (which includes the Holy Spirit as well) was the *key* as well as the *template* for his people's unity. Those united to Jesus the Son are also united to the Father and the Spirit. In Christ they enjoy communion with the triune God!

Though sin alienated us from God and brought deep divisions into the human race, God in Christ has reconciled us to himself and restored the broken relationship. The special work of regeneration changes us so that we are no longer self-centred.[1] As spiritual people we are now able, by God's grace, to lead 'self-controlled, upright and godly lives in the present age' (Titus 2:12).

[1] Martin Luther described sin as making us 'turned in upon ourselves' (*incurvatus in se*), instead of being turned out towards God and others, as God intended us to be.

Paul provides a different angle on this in one of the key exhortations in his letter to the Ephesians: 'Spare no effort to preserve the unity of the Spirit in the bond of peace' (Eph. 4:3).[1] His words here are important for they teach us that the unity of the church is not something *we* synthetically manufacture, but something that has been created within us and between us by God's Spirit in Christ. It is the 'unity *of the Spirit*' and it must be 'maintained'; that is, it must be cherished and guarded by God's people 'in the bond of *peace*' (cf. 1 Thess. 5:13; 2 Tim. 2:22; Heb. 12:14; James 3:18; 1 Pet. 3:11).

Church unity and gospel credibility

Too often Christians have been indifferent to the connection between the church's unity and gospel credibility. The ease with which they separate from other Christians—often over the pettiest of issues—is alarming, given what the apostle Paul commanded in Ephesians 4:3. However, it is even more alarming in the light of the prayer in John 17. In a very emphatic way the Lord makes it clear that he is concerned about more than the unity of his people. First he says in verse 21: 'so that the world may believe that you have sent me'. Then in verse 23 he says: 'so that the world may know that you sent me and loved them even as you loved me'.

The stakes could not be higher. The credibility of the gospel is intimately bound up with the church's unity.

---

[1] Here the translation is my own.

Where there is strife the church's witness will suffer. Sadly we do not have to look far to see the evidence of this. Instead of saying, 'See how they *love* each other,'[1] too often the watching world says, 'See how they *hate* one another.'

Given the weight of the obligation these verses place us under, the closing words of the prayer are all the more crucial, for they give us a glimpse into *how* this unity is to be cultivated: 'I made known to them your name, and I will continue to make it known, that the love with which you have loved me may be in them, and I in them' (John 17:26).

The prayer ends on a similar note to the one on which it began. Jesus had prayed that the Father and Son would be mutually glorified through the giving of eternal life. That life is all about knowing 'you the only true God, and Jesus Christ whom you have sent' (John 17:3). Now we see how deep that knowledge is. It is far, far more than merely knowing *about* God. It is a deep, loving, intimate, experiential knowledge of—*a communion with*—the Father through the Son.

Only as we are drawn deeper into that bond of love with him will we be able to 'maintain the unity of the Spirit in the bond of peace'.

---

[1] An expression used by the North African theologian Tertullian (A.D. 160–220), in his *Apology*.

9

The Church and Its Leaders

Ephesians 4:11-16

For many people church leadership conjures up images of men (and these days, women too!) in clerical garb, performing rituals or representing the church at public events. Such impressions, however, are actually far removed from the kind of leadership we meet in the New Testament church.

From our vantage point we may find the subject of church leadership complicated by many factors. Some of these factors reflect historical developments. The church has so evolved over the centuries that several major streams of church tradition have emerged which are really quite different from each other. For example, at one end of the spectrum there is the 'episcopal' understanding of leadership—consisting of a hierarchy of clergy led from the top by an archbishop, down through different levels of clergy, to the laity in local churches or 'parishes'. At the other end of the spectrum the form of leadership is more 'from the bottom up'. The emphasis is on the congregation choosing its own leaders with no other church body or leader having any say in what happens. Between these two poles is a wide range of other traditions.

Our views of leadership in the church may also be influenced by cultural factors. Every church is shaped to some degree by the culture in which it finds itself. For example, a church (and its view of leadership) in the West is likely to have a different 'flavour' to one in Africa, the Middle East, or Asia.

What is important is to grasp the underlying principles of leadership the Bible teaches and to see the key factors that characterize good leaders in the church, regardless of the particular tradition to which we belong.

Paul's letter to the Ephesians provides some crucial details for understanding leadership in such terms.

Christ's gifts to the church

The apostle lists four types of leader found in the church in New Testament times (Eph. 4:11). Two of them are to be understood as foundational, and therefore unique to the New Testament church—the 'apostles' and 'prophets' mentioned first in the list. They are the foundation on which the church, God's household, is built with 'Christ Jesus himself being the cornerstone' (Eph. 2:20). The foundation of a building is laid at the beginning of the building process, and is laid once and for all; that is why those two special offices are not replicated. God used them to complete his written revelation, our New Testament scriptures, which serves as the underpinning of the church for all time.

The other two offices listed, 'evangelists' and 'pastors and teachers' (or 'pastor-teachers'), have an ongoing role in the growth, instruction, and care of churches.[1]

However, it is important to notice that all four offices (or rather, the men who were entrusted to them) were 'gifts' of the exalted Christ to the church. Through them he provided for the needs of his people.

Although the church has many leaders, it has only one *Leader* in the ultimate sense: the Lord Jesus Christ. He is 'the great shepherd [or pastor] of the sheep' (Heb. 13:20). Though he uses men to feed and care for his flock, it is actually Christ himself who works through them.[2] Those who lead the church only do so under the oversight and supervision of the Lord Jesus, who is 'the head of the body, the church' (Col. 1:18) and 'the Shepherd and Overseer of … souls' (1 Pet. 2:25). Church leaders must not push themselves into office; rather they are to be 'called' into leadership.[3] Church leadership is a *vocation*, not a mere *profession*.

It is also Christ who defines the pattern of leadership.

---

[1] Although John Calvin and others have understood the office of 'evangelist' mentioned here to refer to a special office of men who were 'guardians of the *evangel*' during the New Testament period, others have argued that it should be seen as an enduring office in the church.

[2] We see this in the way Luke begins the Acts of the Apostles as the sequel to the Gospel that bears his name. He speaks of having already written about 'all that *Jesus* began to do and teach, until the day when he was taken up' (Acts 1:1, 2, emphasis added) and so implies that what follows in Acts is the continuation of Jesus' work through the apostles.

[3] Cf. Matt. 4:21; 10:1; Mark 1:20; 6:7; Luke 6:13; 9:1; 1 Cor. 1:1; Gal. 1:15, 16.

We see this principle worked out in the New Testament where specific offices are linked to the work of shepherding and teaching God's people, as well as the ministry of care for the church's more practical needs. These offices fall into two categories—'elder' and 'deacon'. Elders are also described in terms of the work that they undertake in their office—as 'pastors' and 'overseers'. The elder has two distinct but overlapping functions: one is teaching, the other is shepherding God's sheep. The Lord's provision of elders and deacons ensures that God's people will be well taught and cared for both spiritually and practically.

Equipped for service

The church's leaders are not to be isolated from the people for whom they care. Paul tells the Ephesians that the purpose for which Christ has given pastors and teachers is 'to equip the saints for the work of ministry, for building up the body of Christ, until we all attain to the unity of the faith and of the knowledge of the Son of God, to mature manhood, to the measure of the stature of the fullness of Christ' (Eph. 4:12, 13).

Christ calls into his service men who are 'fit for purpose'. He gives them the necessary qualities and abilities to fulfil their responsibilities of office. In his letters to Timothy and Titus Paul supplies further instructions about qualifications for office (1 Tim. 3:1-13; Titus 1:6-9). It is striking to see how strong the emphasis is on personal character and the leader's relationship to his family and the wider community. The ability to teach or lead the church depends on a man being not only a Christian, but a well-rounded human being who is able to relate to others.

These personal qualities and interpersonal skills should never be minimized in the church's assessment of a man's suitability for office. Whatever gifts and abilities he may have, a leader needs the kind of Christian character and gracious spirit that will enable him to win the respect of others and to teach, pastor, and lead those entrusted to his care. Paul supplies his colleague Timothy with a representative sample of these personal characteristics: elders and deacons must be known for their self-control, hospitality, and gentleness (1 Tim. 3:1-13).

There are, of course, other gifts necessary for the task of leading churches. For those whose primary calling is to preach and teach, the ability to understand God's word accurately and to handle it faithfully is essential (2 Tim. 2:15). Those called to care for the pastoral needs of God's people must have the requisite wisdom, gentleness, and interpersonal skills.

Gifts given and received need to be continually improved by disciplined exercise. Paul tells Timothy to 'fan into flame the gift of God, which is in you' (2 Tim. 1:6), and with respect to the various tasks of a preaching and teaching ministry, he must 'practise these things, devote [himself] to them, so that all may see [his] progress' (1 Tim. 4:15). Therefore, full use needs to be made of the gifts the Lord has given—whether to pastors and teachers, elders or deacons—and the gifts need to be nurtured and developed.

To build up the church

The goal of church leadership is not to enhance the leader's reputation, but to build up the church as the body of Christ (Eph. 4:12). Peter exhorts his fellow elders to

> shepherd the flock of God that is among you, exercising oversight, not under compulsion, but willingly, as God would have you; not for shameful gain, but eagerly; not domineering over those in your charge, but being examples to the flock (1 Pet. 5:2, 3).

Leaders are not to serve simply because they must, or because of greed, or because they want to 'lord it over' the people. Rather they are to see themselves as *servants*, who serve willingly as 'examples to the flock'. Their gifts and abilities have been given, not for their own self-advancement, but for the benefit of the church.

As the elders lead and shepherd the people in accordance with the calling they have received, their service will enable the church to grow into richer and deeper communion with God and with one another. Christ will so nourish every part of his body that it will not only grow but build itself up in love (Eph. 4:15, 16).

Addressing the Ephesian elders in a different context, Paul gave them a solemn exhortation which is also a remarkable summary of what is involved in leading Christ's church: 'Pay careful attention to yourselves and to all the flock, of which the Holy Spirit has made you overseers, to care for the church of God, which he obtained with his own blood' (Acts 20:28). The work of an elder is a high calling and a noble task (cf. 1 Tim. 3:1). Overcome with a sense of the greatness of the work and a sense of personal inadequacy, many have found themselves asking with Paul: 'Who is sufficient for these things?' (2 Cor. 2:16). Humanly speaking, the answer is 'No one!' But when church leaders realize what they are in Christ and what he graciously supplies, then, again with Paul, they can say, 'I can do all things through him who strengthens me' (Phil. 4:13).

10

The Church and the World

Matthew 5:13-16

The relationship between the church and the world has always involved tension. The Greek word[1] used for 'world' in the New Testament often has the sense of 'everything that is opposed to God, his people, and his work'. The world is a hostile environment for the church.

The church has frequently struggled to define its relationship to the world. Sometimes it has adopted a policy of retreat from the world. The monastic movement of the medieval period, for example, was a well-intentioned effort to protect Christians from the world's sinful influences. It was thought that Christians could somehow escape the temptations and pressures of the world by taking refuge behind the high walls of monasteries and convents. They soon discovered, however, that temptations were just as real and ever-present a danger within the peaceful surroundings of these religious sanctuaries as they were outside.

More frequently, however, the church accommodated itself to the world. Instead of standing against the tide of

[1] *Kosmos.*

secular influences and the various attempts made to dis-credit Christian doctrine, principles and ethics, the church simply redefined itself in order to minimize conflict with the world. Neither the policy of retreat or accommoda-tion reflects the teaching of Scripture on church–world relations.

In the Lord Jesus Christ we not only have his clear teach-ing on the nature of this relationship, but we also have the embodiment of it in his own life and interactions with the world in its various forms. The apostle John tells us that Jesus 'was in the world' (John 1:10). It was in our fallen and sinful world that he 'dwelt among us' and revealed his glory (John 1:14). Jesus did not spend his time here in hermetically sealed isolation; instead, he engaged with people in all the foul ugliness of their sin. But though he was *in* the world he was not *of* it. The same can be said of all those who are united to him by faith, as we learn from what Jesus said in his prayer to his Father: '*They* are not of the world, just as *I* am not of the world' (John 17:16). Jesus not only defines the relationship that exists between his people and the world, but, at the same time, he displays how that relationship is worked out in practice.

The Lord's teaching on the relationship his people are to have with the world is perhaps most clearly seen in the Sermon on the Mount, in which he tells his disciples that they are 'the salt of the earth' and 'the light of the world' (Matt. 5:13-16).

The salt of the earth

Salt had many important functions in the ancient world. In some cultures it was used as currency. But its most common use, especially in hot Mediterranean countries, was as a preservative for food. In conditions that accelerated decay in fish, meat and poultry, salt was used to prolong the 'shelf-life' of these items.

The church's presence in a morally corrupt world will have a restraining influence on sin and evil. Simply by being 'in the world, but not of it', God's people will make their presence felt—not just because of what they do or don't do, but because of *what they are*. People who are made new in Christ cannot help being 'different' from those around them; they *are* different. It is inevitable that their new life in Christ and the conduct that flows out from it will challenge the very different lifestyle of the world around them. In that sense they will be something of an irritant, as irritating, perhaps, as salt in a wound! Or, to change the metaphor, as Christians draw the straight line of their new life in Christ alongside the crooked line of the lives of the worldly people around them, they cannot help but uncover the ugly character of godless lives.

At times the sinfulness of the world needs to be challenged directly. When certain expressions of sin have become so ingrained that they are accepted in society, the church must speak out against them. There have been significant periods in history when the church has vigorously opposed social and moral evils. Its role in the anti-slavery movement, prison reform, and the campaign to introduce humane industrial working conditions are instances of the church proactively rubbing salt into the putrefying wounds of the world.

Although the 'salt metaphor' has seemingly negative connotations, J. I. Packer has pointed out that salt is also used to bring flavour to otherwise bland food. The presence of Christians in the world should make it a 'tastier' place to live in. If we were to undertake a survey of all the benefits local communities and even whole countries received when large numbers of their people became Christians, Packer's point would be most clearly demonstrated.

The light of the world

The second metaphor Jesus used of the church is unquestionably positive: 'You are the light of the world. A city set on a hill cannot be hidden' (Matt. 5:14). The church is not only to expose the wrong that corrupts the world in which it lives, it is also to proclaim and be an example of the right.

If we are to grasp the implications of Jesus' teaching here, then we need to understand what lies at the heart of this particular role of light-bearing.

One of the most significant, but arguably the most destructive, eras in the history of human thought was the so-called 'Age of Enlightenment'. It began around the latter part of the seventeenth century but reached its height in the late eighteenth. Its proponents elevated human reason to a whole new level, and, in doing so, marginalized God in the whole process. This 'enlightenment' was very different from what Jesus had in mind when he spoke of 'light' and the church being 'the light of the world'. Far from relegating God to the periphery of human thought, Jesus taught that the God who has made himself known in Scripture is to be acknowledged as the vital element in human knowledge and understanding. As Solomon put it: 'the fear of the LORD is the beginning of knowledge', and 'wisdom' too (Prov. 1:7; 9:10).

Jesus Christ himself is the key to true knowledge and wisdom. He is 'the light of the world' (John 8:12; 9:5). He is light because he is none other than the Son of God in human flesh, who uniquely reveals God to the world. That is why he could say to his disciples: 'Whoever has seen me has seen the Father' (John 14:9).

If the church is to function as 'the light of the world' it must be totally dependent on Jesus Christ. To be in Christ, to have the word of Christ, to be empowered by the Spirit of Christ is the only way the church can live and speak for him in a world that is morally and spiritually darkness itself. The church has exercised its greatest influence over the nations when it has lived in close communion with Christ. When revived by the Spirit and reformed according to the word of God, the church has been instrumental in the transformation of nations. However, sad to say, there have also been times when the church, though institutionally and numerically strong, has utterly failed to make a lasting impression on society.

Jesus told his disciples to let their light shine before men—not to hide it or to dim its brightness—but to let it shine; for when the light shines brightly, the people of the world will see the church's good works and glorify the Father in heaven (Matt. 5:16).

Between two worlds

Undergirding all that Jesus says on the subject of the church and the world is a massive truth which runs like a seam through the whole Bible. Often it lies just under the surface, but every now and again the biblical writers bring it to the surface.

For example, Paul mentions it in his first letter to the Corinthians. The Christians in Corinth struggled to make sense of who they were and how they fitted into this confused and confusing world. Paul tells them they are those 'on whom the end of the ages has come' (1 Cor. 10:11). In other words, at that particular juncture in God's redemptive purpose, they were witnessing the dawn of a new epoch in the history of the world in which God was dealing with the human race in a new way.

Even though the old order of this fallen and rebellious world is still a reality, a new and infinitely greater order has been introduced with the coming of Christ. Paul wanted the Corinthians to understand that the tensions they were feeling, and the perplexities with which they struggled, all stemmed from the fact they were living at the crossroads of the ages, the interface between two worlds.

On the one hand, they were 'in Corinth', still living in the world that is under God's curse and passing away. But at the same time, they were 'in Christ', members of a new world—part of the new creation—under the Lordship of Jesus Christ, the God-appointed and God-sent Saviour. The Christians in Corinth were to orientate their lives in this world according to the principles and the laws of that better world of which they were citizens.

The tensions of living in this 'already, but not yet'[1] period are as real today as they were in the apostle's day. It is only as the church holds firmly to God's truth, realizing that she belongs to the world to come, that she will fulfil her calling to be 'the salt of the earth' and 'the light of the world'.

---

[1] Geerhardus Vos (1862–1949), Professor of Biblical Theology in Princeton Theological Seminary, coined this expression as a means of understanding that although Christians live in this age, they belong to the age to come.

11

The Church and Its Failures

Revelation 2:1–3:22

The *Westminster Confession of Faith* pulls no punches when it states:

> The purest churches under heaven are subject both to mixture and error; and some have so degenerated, as to become no churches of Christ, but synagogues of Satan. Nevertheless, there shall be always a church on earth to worship God according to his will.[1]

Despite the glorious future God has planned for the church in the world to come, its life in this present world will always be tarnished by sin and failure. As one writer has put it: 'The affairs of the church at their very best are always a sanctified mess!'

The story of the church is at times embarrassing to read. The pages of the Old Testament contain some shocking things. How quickly and with what ease did God's people turn away from him to sin. The book of Judges contains many examples of Israel's spiritual and moral declension.

---

[1] *Westminster Confession of Faith*, XXV.5.

But lest we be tempted to get on our high horse and con-demn this sinful behaviour, we ought to remember the warning given to the Corinthians: 'let anyone who thinks that he stands take heed lest he fall' (1 Cor. 10:12).

The New Testament church, as we have often seen in our studies so far, was not without its failures. The little 'congregation' that Jesus pastored even had a member who was 'a devil' (John 6:70)! Many of the New Testament letters were written to churches which, even under the leadership of the apostles, had their fair share of failures!

Perhaps the saddest insight into this aspect of the church's life is found in the book of Revelation. Yet this last book of the Bible also sets out the church's greatest hope.

The Lord Jesus commanded his servant John to write letters to seven churches in the province of Asia (Rev. 2:1–3:22). The letters show us what Christ really thinks of them and contain his loving but robust critique. But they are written in such a way as to provide a litmus test for the spiritual health of the whole church. While they give us a perspective on the actual failures of real churches in the first century A.D., they also provide a representative survey of defects which have marred the church throughout history.

The sad reality of failure

But before we look at this passage in more detail, we should keep in mind some words written by the apostle John to individual Christians in his first letter (which was probably a circular communiqué sent round a group of churches under his care near Ephesus in the same province of Asia). He wrote: 'If we say we have no sin, we deceive ourselves, and the truth is not in us … If we say we have not sinned, we make him [God] a liar, and his word is not in us' (1 John 1:8, 10). Such strong statements as these needed to be made because, as the rest of his letter points out, many churches in that region had embraced a certain kind of false teaching which claimed Christians could be free from sin in this life. 'No!' says John, 'such a position is not true to Scripture and does not reflect true Christian experience. It is a self-deceiving error to say that we have no sin or that we have not sinned. It goes against what God has said in his word.'

Paul expresses the same truth in a candid word of personal testimony. He speaks of sin as something that persists in the life of a Christian, and he illustrates from his own experience. With breathtaking honesty he confesses: 'I do not do what I want, but I do the very thing I hate', and by way of explanation he adds: 'it is no longer I who do it, but sin that dwells within me' (Rom. 7:15, 17). Indeed, he even says: 'Wretched man that I am! Who will deliver me from this body of death? Thanks be to God through Jesus Christ our Lord!' (Rom. 7:24, 25).

The Bible is unequivocal about 'indwelling sin' that lurks in the hearts of all God's children. It distorts our thinking and contaminates the very best obedience we offer to God. But, as Paul confessed, Jesus Christ is the divinely provided and never-failing antidote to this running sore in our Christian experience.

As we 'listen in' to Christ's spiritual State of the Union Address to this cluster of seven churches in first-century Asia Minor we cannot help but notice a recurring theme—the church's need to face up to ongoing failure. Although it may seem like a contradiction in terms, we need to realize that there is no shame in acknowledging that the church will always be plagued with failure in this present world. For only as she recognizes this sad reality will she truly appreciate and love her Saviour.

The consequences of failure

In the seven letters the Lord Jesus Christ not only identifies the specific sins of individual churches, but also warns them what will happen if their sins are not dealt with properly. For example, he warns the church at Pergamum that if it does not deal with those in their congregation who 'hold the teaching of Balaam' (Rev. 2:14), he himself will 'war against them with the sword of [his] mouth' (Rev. 2:16). He warns the Laodiceans, whom he describes as 'lukewarm, and neither hot nor cold', that he will spew them out of his mouth if they do not turn from their sinful indifference of heart (Rev. 3:16). Any church that refuses to heed his warning is threatened with the removal of its lampstand (Rev. 2:5). It is sobering to think that this region of the Mediterranean became a spiritual wilderness totally bereft of gospel churches for centuries. The lesson is stark: no church can afford to ignore the warnings!

The way back

The beauty of the gospel of grace is that God never speaks words of warning and judgment without also speaking words of mercy and grace. That was true for Adam and Eve in the Garden (Gen. 3:15), for Noah at the flood (Gen. 8:20-22), and it has been the pattern of God's dealings with sinners ever since. Though Christ speaks words of warning to the seven churches of Asia, he does not leave them without a promise of forgiveness and restoration. Time and again he tells such wayward churches: 'He who has an ear, let him hear what the Spirit says to the churches' (Rev. 2:7, 11, 17, 29; 3:6, 13, 22). The 'hearing' Jesus has in mind is that which leads to an obedient response. He speaks of *repentance*. What he says to the church in Ephesus sets the tone for them all: 'repent, and do the works you did at first' (Rev. 2:5; cf. 2:16, 22).

Christ's most winsome call to repentance is found in his words to the church at Laodicea:

> Behold, I stand at the door and knock. If anyone hears my voice and opens the door, I will come in to him and eat with him, and he with me (Rev. 3:20).

This is a picture of Jesus calling upon those who claim to be his people to open the door of their church to him and let him in. The promise he extends to the one who hears his voice and opens the door is that of table fellowship. This is a vivid and heart-warming picture. It is a portrayal of the restoration of communion with Jesus, a communion which is so richly experienced by the believer in the Lord's Supper.

12

The Church and Its Sufferings

1 Peter 1:3-9; 4:12-19

Suffering is one of the great enigmas of life. That is universally true for 'man is born to trouble as the sparks fly upward' (Job 5:7). All of us struggle to cope with life's problems and make sense of them. But that is perhaps especially true for Christians. Their struggle with pain and sorrow takes on a unique complexion, not least because they have put their faith in a *good* God who is in *sovereign control* of all things. And therein lies the problem.

The Bible does not ignore this. It has one entire book[1] devoted to what theologians call 'theodicy'—an understanding of the relationship between God and suffering. Other significant sections of the Bible deal with this issue also. The prophets wrestle with it in the messages they bring from God. The book of Psalms contains numerous songs which touch on the sufferings of God's people.[2]

---

[1] The book of Job in the Old Testament.

[2] The standpoint of these psalms brings us great benefit in that they not only speak *to* us in our pain, but they also speak *for* us—supplying us with words to say in prayer when we struggle to find words of our own.

The Bible gives us an even more salient perspective on suffering in what it reveals concerning the Lord Jesus Christ as the incarnate Son of God. The Old Testament prophecies revealed that the coming Messiah would know suffering and sorrow (Isa. 53:3). Indeed, Isaiah speaks of him as the Suffering Servant of the Lord. Many psalms open our ears to the Saviour's cries in the midst of his sufferings on earth. David's words in Psalm 22 are a vivid example. Jesus took the poignant cry of this psalm upon his lips while hanging on the cross (Matt. 27:46). The New Testament presses home the truth that Jesus was indeed the 'man of sorrows' who was 'acquainted with grief'.

Suffering has never been far from the church's experience. Jesus left his followers in no doubt about this when he gave them their final briefing. He told them straight: 'In the world you will have tribulation' (John 16:33).

Many parts of Scripture throw light on this dark and painful subject, but what Peter says in his first letter is of particular significance. He was writing to Christians who had been scattered because of persecution.[1] They had experienced a period of severe distress which was far from over. Shepherding them from a distance by letter, Peter wanted to help them understand what they were going through so that they would not only survive their sufferings but actually grow as a result of them.

---

[1] Cf. the comments in chapter 1.

A necessary part of discipleship

'Beloved, do not be surprised at the fiery trial when it comes upon you to test you, as though something strange were happening to you' (1 Pet. 4:12). No doubt the Christians were surprised, if not by the opposition itself, then perhaps by its intensity and persistence. But Peter is reminding them of the terms Jesus laid down in his gospel invitation: 'If anyone would come after me, let him deny himself and *take up his cross* and follow me' (Mark 8:34). The call to discipleship is a call to a life of suffering. 'When Christ calls a man, he bids him come and die.'[1]

It would be wrong to interpret Jesus' words as implying that the Christian life is one of gratuitous suffering. Rather, the point he was making is that to belong to his kingdom is to be caught up in a conflict. It is the same idea to which Paul referred in his first letter to the Corinthians about Christians being those 'on whom the end of the ages has come' (1 Cor. 10:11).[2] Just as the fault lines that separate the tectonic plates of the earth's crust are the cause of violent earthquakes, so opposition and persecution are caused by the colliding of the spiritual tectonic plates of the kingdom of light and the kingdom of darkness. And that friction translates into the various sufferings Christians experience.

---

[1] A quote from the writings of Dietrich Bonhoeffer (1906–45), a German Lutheran pastor, theologian, participant in the German resistance movement against Nazism, and founding member of the Confessing Church.

[2] Cf. chapter 10.

Even though there is a general experience of suffering for everyone and everything in this fallen world and universe (because of Adam's sin and God's ensuing curse upon creation, Gen. 3:8-19), that suffering takes on a distinct dimension for those who are in Christ.

God's purpose in his people's pain

The inevitable questions that ring out from God's suffering people are, 'Why?' and 'How long, O Lord?' We hear them repeatedly in the Psalms as well as in other parts of the Bible. Our Lord himself, in a way that is shrouded in mystery, cried out '*Why?*' in the darkest moment of his sufferings on the cross (Matt. 27:46).

Peter answers this question for the church by saying that trials come 'so that the tested genuineness of your faith—more precious than gold that perishes though it is tested by fire—may be found to result in praise and glory and honour at the revelation of Jesus Christ' (1 Pet. 1:7). James says something similar in his letter to Christians who were facing the same sort of struggles as those addressed by Peter (cf. James 1:2-4).

The church's sufferings are neither beyond God's control, nor outside his wise and loving purpose. They are, in effect, like the refiner's fire that burns off the dross and that purifies the gold. Although God does not often deliver his people from these trials, he promises to bring them through them and out the other side. By his sanctifying grace they shall be bettered by the experience (cf. Heb. 12:4-13).

Peter gives another insight into God's purpose in these dark circumstances of life. Sufferings bring us to an end of ourselves so that we learn to depend on God more fully for all our needs. See how the apostle ends the second major section of his letter on suffering with these words: 'Therefore let those who suffer according to God's will *entrust their souls to a faithful Creator* while doing good' (1 Pet. 4:19). Far from being something that restricts the church's growth and development, suffering, if approached in this way, will promote its progress.

Suffering and the church's testimony

Christians are by no means the only people who suffer in this world, but the Bible makes it clear that the way they bear their sufferings will mark them out as being different. This is something Peter wants his suffering readers to fully grasp.

God's people face suffering *with joy*. The harsh reality of what they suffer in this world does not diminish their joy in God's great gospel (1 Pet. 1:6). Indeed, even in the dark valley of pain believers may yet 'rejoice with joy that is inexpressible and filled with glory' (1 Pet. 1:8).

James puts an even sharper point on this lesson when he says: '*Count it all joy*, my brothers, when you meet trials of various kinds' (James 1:2). Is that even possible? Yes, it is, as we see it demonstrated in the case of Paul and Silas at Philippi. In that city they were arrested, flogged, and thrown into prison without a trial. But rather than complain against God and feel sorry for themselves in their dungeon, they offered up prayers and sang hymns of praise to God. What a witness that must have been to their fellow prisoners (Acts 16:25)! Paul and Silas were simply taking the Lord Jesus at his word and putting into practice what they had learned from his Sermon on the Mount: 'Blessed are you when others revile you and persecute you and utter all kinds of evil against you falsely on my account. *Rejoice and be glad*, for your reward is great in heaven' (Matt. 5:11-12).

God's people endure suffering *with patience*. Peter reminds them that however intense their trials may be, or however long they may endure, in God's grand scheme of things, they are only 'for a little while' (1 Pet. 1:6). Or, as Paul put it: 'I consider that the sufferings of this present time are not worth comparing with the glory that is to be revealed to us' (Rom. 8:18). It is this perspective that enables Christians to be 'patient in tribulation' (Rom. 12:12).

It is fascinating to see how Peter connects suffering and witnessing by telling his readers: 'if you should suffer for righteousness' sake … always [be] prepared to make a defence to anyone who asks you for a reason for the hope that is in you' (1 Pet. 3:14-15). Handling our sufferings in the right way—joyfully and patiently—will open doors of opportunity for the gospel that would otherwise remain firmly closed.

13

The Church and Its Future

Revelation 21:1-8

The Bible begins with a broken engagement but ends with a marriage. Adam and Eve, created by God for a unique relationship with him, were placed in the perfect environment of the Garden of Eden and 'betrothed', as it were, to God. They were put under one simple, but far-reaching obligation: to demonstrate their love for God by 'forsaking all others and cleaving only unto him'. Hence God's single prohibition: not to eat from the only tree in the Garden he had placed out of bounds. However, instead of proving their devotion to God, Adam and Eve rebelled against him.

The Scriptures reveal the plan God made and the steps he took to redeem his fallen race. The story is a roller-coaster romance—at least from the perspective of the fickle bride. Those who read the story may well wonder if the bride will 'make it to the altar'. It is not just that she is 'tempted, tried and *sometimes* failing' as one hymn writer put it;[1] but that she is 'tempted, tried and *always* failing'.

---

[1] From the hymn 'Jesus! What a Friend for Sinners!', J. Wilbur Chapman (1859–1918).

Even though the promise is written on every page that his purpose will not be thwarted, it is only when we reach the last book of the Bible that we see its ultimate fulfilment.

The title of the last book in the Bible—'Revelation'—comes from the Greek word for 'unveiling'. In a very real sense the book uncovers something that we would never be able to see if left to our own devices. While it shows us some aspects of the future, it mainly gives us a glimpse into the inner workings of God's plan of salvation and where it will ultimately lead.

The book of Revelation was written for a troubled church which had been ravaged from *outside* by persecution and from *inside* by many kinds of failure. It was written to encourage believers and to reassure them of God's unwavering commitment to his promises.

The perfect church in a perfect world

The practice of sending postcards while on vacation is not as common as it once was in the pre-digital age. Nevertheless when people send postcards, the picture on the front is designed to convey the message, 'Wish you were here!' This, in effect, is what John did, who wrote the book of Revelation while exiled on the small island of Patmos in the eastern Aegean Sea. The message of this 'picture postcard' of heaven which he sent could hardly have been more alluring. The old apostle's eyes had been opened to see beyond the present discouraging circumstances of the church. The Lord Jesus was giving him a vision of the church's future. And it was a glorious sight!

Instead of a world that was weary, worn and sad from the effects of the fall (Rom. 8:20-21), John saw a 'new' heaven and earth (Rev. 21:1)—not new in the sense of being completely different from the world we know at present, but new in the sense of the utter renovation of that same world (2 Pet. 3:10-13). The church—portrayed symbolically as the city of Jerusalem—will be 'holy' and 'new' (Rev. 21:2). And since there was no longer any sea in the vision given to John, nothing would ever shake, disturb or threaten God's new order.[1]

The imagery then changes from a city to 'a bride adorned for her husband' on her wedding day (Rev. 21:2). Her beauty is not that of a stunning dress or of cosmetics that hide her natural blemishes. Instead, she is intrinsically perfect in every way. In fact, the wedding takes place on the day when God brings every one of his covenant promises to fulfilment. A loud voice is heard from heaven, declaring: 'Behold, the dwelling place of God is with man. He will dwell with them, and they will be his people, and God himself will be with them as their God' (Rev. 21:3).

To underscore the point, John uses a number of negatives in this little cameo of the future: there will be no more tears, death, mourning, crying or pain (Rev. 21:4). Everything that reflects the pain and misery of life in this

---

[1] John is either speaking metaphorically about the real sea surrounding his tiny island that cut him off from his fellow Christians, or else he was using the sea, as the Old Testament sometimes does, to symbolize the ever-present unrest and chaos that permeates this present world.

world, even at its very best, will be gone, 'for the former things have passed away' (Rev. 21:4). More than that, the unrepentant, sin-hardened people and the sins they love to commit will be removed and for ever banished from this new order (Rev. 21:8).

The apostle goes on to give yet another perspective on God's 'perfected' community. He describes the church in terms of precious jewels and he speaks of a city of extraordinary dimensions (Rev. 21.9-21). Once more his intent is not to give a literal description. He is using the most striking and vivid language at his disposal to emphasize the priceless worth of God's people—secured at the infinite cost of the precious blood of Christ. They are the 'crown jewels' and will be kept in the impregnable fortress of God himself.

God as the centre of his new creation

The church's beauty and splendour are not her own, but gifts that come from God (Rev. 21:10, 11). Like a mirror without a crack or a smudge, the church is God's earthly 'mirror-image'—now saved and perfected for all to see and admire.

This theme of glory is taken further in the details that follow. There will be no temple in this new order, because God's fellowship with his people will finally come into its own. Although the bond of union between God and his people will be no stronger in the future than it is now in the present, their enjoyment of communion with him in that relationship will reach its zenith.

Since God will be acknowledged and worshipped by men and angels, perfect order will be restored in his universe. 'Everything will be as it should be with nothing out of place'.[1] The great 'shalom' or 'peace' that defines the very essence of the blessing God promised to his ancient people[2] will characterize everything.

An open invitation to a whole new life

God in all his glory as Father, Son and Holy Spirit dominates the entire landscape of the new heavens and the new earth. And yet God's glory does not completely eclipse the glory of the church. In this we see how God delights to turn the spotlight on the church to display her in all her glory as his 'new creation' in Christ.

Perhaps the most glorious thing of all is that God and his bride join their voices together to pronounce a final word of gospel invitation to the very world that has risen up against them both.

> The Spirit and the Bride say, 'Come.' And let the one who hears say, 'Come.' And let the one who is thirsty come; let the one who desires take the water of life without price (Rev. 22:17).

This wonderful, gracious, warm, and earnest free offer of salvation stands out even more clearly by being set against the sober warning that follows, directed against

---

[1] The definition favoured by Rev. Dr Stuart Sacks, a Jewish believer and former colleague of mine in Proclamation Presbyterian Church, Bryn Mawr, PA.

[2] Cf. Num. 6:24-26.

those who will stubbornly refuse to believe the gospel and receive what Christ alone can give (Rev. 22:18-19).

Could there be a more poignant yet appropriate note on which God's message to a fallen world could end? The God against whom Adam rebelled at the very beginning of time is the same God who graciously offers mercy to Adam's rebellious race at the very end. And he does so in concert with his church.

When the world sees the church as Christ's 'glorious body and radiant bride', and hears from her lips the gospel of salvation entrusted to her, then it will be God who truly receives the glory. That has been his purpose from the start.

Further Reading

Where to start

Dale Ralph Davis, *The House That Jesus Built* (Christian Focus Publications, 2015)

Mark Dever, *The Church: the Gospel Made Visible* (B & H Publishing, 2012)

Jonathan Leeman, *Church Membership* (Crossway, 2012)

Sean Michael Lucas, *What Is Church Government?* (P & R Publishing, 2009)

Richard D. Phillips, *What Is the Lord's Supper?* (P & R Publishing, 2005)

Stephen Smallman, *What Is a Reformed Church?* (P & R Publishing, 2012)

In more detail

E. P. Clowney, *The Church* (IVP, 1995)

R. B. Kuiper, *The Glorious Body of Christ* (Banner of Truth Trust, 1966)

Richard D. Phillips, *The Church: One, Holy and Apostolic* (P & R Publishing, 2004)

Philip G. Ryken, *City on a Hill* (Moody Publishers, 2003)

Philip G. Ryken, *The Communion of Saints* (P & R Publishing, 2001)

The bigger picture

James Bannerman, *The Church of Christ* (Banner of Truth Trust, 2015)

Herman Bavinck, *Holy Spirit, Church and New Creation*; *Reformed Dogmatics*, vol. 4 (Baker Academic, 2008)